Revised Edition

EASY, EASIER, EASIEST
TAILORING
by
pati palmer & susan pletsch

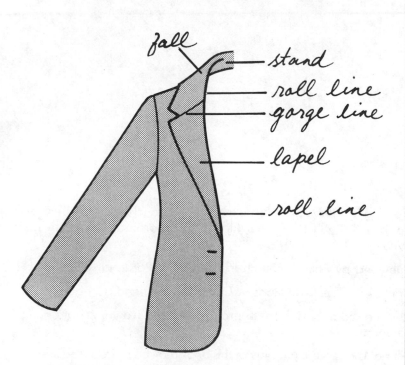

fall

stand

roll line

gorge line

lapel

roll line

cover & fashion illustrations by Priscilla F. Lee

Whenever brand names are mentioned, it is only to indicate to the consumer products we have personally tested and with which we have been pleased. There may very well be other products that are comparable or even better to aid you in your sewing or that may be developed after the printing of this book.

A special thank you to our innovative friend, Marta Alto, and to our families who have been supportive fans.

About the authors . . . . . .

Pati Palmer and Susan Pletsch, two talented home economists, have developed careers promoting a favorite hobby, home sewing. They have co-authored four sewing books, have established their own publishing company, and now travel across the U.S. teaching seminars based on Palmer/Pletsch books. They also consult with fabric and notion companies. Their most recent accomplishments include designing patterns for McCall's and Vogue and creating and starring in an educational film based on a Palmer/Pletsch book.

Pati and Susan met as educational representatives for Armo, a shaping fabrics manufacturer. Pati has also been Corporate Home Economist for an Oregon department store, as well as buyer of sewing notions. Pati graduated from Oregon State University with a B.S. in Home Economics. She is active in the American Home Economics Association, Home Economists in Business, and Fashion Group.

Pati Palmer

Susan has been a home economist with Talon Consumer Education, where she traveled extensively giving workshops. She was also a free-lance home economist with many sewing related firms. Susan graduated from Arizona State University in home economics and taught home economics to special education students. She is active in the American Home Economics Association and Home Economists in Business.

Susan Pletsch

Pati and Susan are individually recognized for their sewing skills and teaching and lecturing abilities. Together they produce an unbeatable combination of knowledge, personality and talent.

Table of Contents

Tailoring Is EASY!

Can you believe it? We have the nerve to call tailoring EASY! And we mean it. We began as you did, "Me tailor? Heavens no — that's too hard for me!" But tailoring can be as easy as **you** want it to be. That's what this book is all about.

We've written a book full of choices. You must evaluate your time, talent, patience, budget, and wardrobe plans and then choose tailoring methods to meet your needs. So you can be a snob and "custom" tailor if that is your choice. But you will also find some sneaky, speedy ways to have a great looking blazer in 1/4 the time with 1/4 the hassle. Using the "Easiest" methods, we can crank one out in 8 hours — and YOU can too!

Read the entire book first! Then . . . **think** positively, your new blazer is going to make Calvin Klein think he needs sewing lessons! **Decide** which methods meet your talents and needs. **Plan** your work so that it will progress smoothly and rapidly. Then **smile** and pat yourself on the back. Isn't tailoring easy!

What Makes It "Tailored"?

"Tailoring" is a method of sewing that makes a garment more durable than traditional dressmaking. It generally applies to coats, jackets, and blazers — those garments that cost more to buy or sew — those garments we must wear for several seasons. "Tailored" can also refer to a "man-tailored" fashion look (crisp details, masculine fabrics, man's suit styling) which can be found on anything from skirts to dresses to pants.

A blazer, which we define as a type of jacket that always has a lapel, a rolled collar, and a straight, uncuffed sleeve, contains virtually all of the traditional techniques that set tailoring apart from dressmaking. You may find one or more of the following tailoring techniques in a tailored jacket or coat, but if you want to learn **all** about tailoring, make a blazer — it has them all!

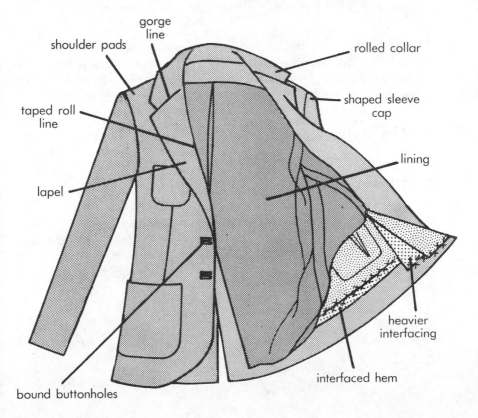

Why Learn Tailoring Techniques?

1.   If you learn to tailor, all of your sewing will improve because you will have tried and succeeded with the psychologically most difficult sewing project. It's much like the novice skier who dares to tackle the advanced slope and succeeds — one must put forth maximum effort and use every bit of previous training and knowledge. From that point on, skiing is a breeze!

2.   You can make your sewing time as profitable as possible by making only those things you can't afford to buy. Susan says she can afford $15.00 T-shirts but refuses to spend $200.00 for the quality blazer she loves. She multiplies the cost of the blazer ingredients by 7 to come up with the approximate cost of a comparable ready-to-wear garment. With $40.00 worth of ingredients you can produce a $280.00 blazer — a savings of $240.00! Tailoring can save tons of money!

3.   You will have the skill to produce classic garments to wear for many seasons. You will have the advantage of achieving perfect fit in just the right fabric (neither is always available in ready-to-wear!) and to create that important wardrobe core — the jacket.

4.   Special tailoring techniques can be used for super effects in sewing many other garments. For example, the taping technique taught on page 54 can be used to prevent "gaposis" on the V-neck of a daring evening dress.

5.   Because fashion constantly changes, learning classic tailoring methods will prepare you to sew any new fashion look. For example, bound buttonholes have been passé lately. Designers have replaced them with a sportier keyhole style, but we guarantee bound buttonholes will return!

Let's Define: Easy, Easier, Easiest

Custom — Totally Hand Stitched

- Hand tailor baste hair canvas interfacing to front
- Hand pad stitch lapels
- Underlining is optional
- Best quality fabrics are suggested due to time invested

Advantages: Subtle, durable shape with all fabrics.
Disadvantages: Very slow. Hand stitches can show on smooth, lightweight fabrics.

Easy — Machine Replaces Some Hand Stitching

- Must use an underlining
- Machine stitch hair canvas to underlining
- Hand or glue baste underlining to fashion fabric
- Hand pad stitch lapels

Advantages: Faster than custom, durable — great for children's coats; can use a budget hair canvas
Disadvantages: Underlining plus interfacing may be too bulky or firm for some fabrics

Easier — Fuse to Underlining

- Must use an underlining
- Fuse interfacing to underlining
- Hand or glue baste underlining to fashion fabric

Advantages: Speedy, yet gives extra body; a way to use fusibles on any fabric without creating ridges on outside or altering fabric surface — Great for seersucker!
Disadvantages: Underlining plus interfacing may be too bulky for some fabrics.

Easiest — Fuse to Fabric

- Fuse a fusible interfacing directly to fashion fabric
- No underlining
- No machine or hand pad stitches

Advantages: SPEED! Adds body and wrinkle-resistance. Fusibles are available in many weights.
Disadvantages: Must stock a variety of fusibles at home to make test samples; some fusibles adhere to some fabrics better than others.

Think Coordinates —
Sew an OUTFIT

Spend more time but get better value from your time spent — don't just make a jacket or coat — make an outfit!

Save Time

1. **Make a two-piece outfit** — That is, make a grey blazer and grey skirt or a camel coat and pants. There is super classic fashion in a monochromatic ensemble and definitely extra wardrobe mileage.

2. **Go one step further** — make a blazer, vest, skirt and pants out of the same fabric. This four part wardrobe can yield many more combinations.

3. **Go even further** — make two four-piece outfits out of a year-round fabric like a stretch woven polyester in two compatible colors (such as camel and navy), and you can interchange all the parts. The two outfits then yield over 25 combinations. Pati always has these two colors in her wardrobe and builds all other garments around them.

> **NOTE:** When you make a two, three or four-piece outfit, make the "other pieces" (vest or skirt or pants) first to become familiar with the fashion fabric — how it presses, how it sews.

Save Money

1. **On fabric** — by buying enough fabric for a 3-piece outfit, you can often make the fourth piece for free because of improved cutting advantages.

2. **On other clothes** — fewer blouses, shirts and sweaters will compliment more outfits.

3. **On accessories** — when you have all those compatible pieces you can wear the same shoes, handbag, scarves and jewelry. (This also means you save time in shopping for your accessories).

> **NOTE:** Carry color swatches with you! Buy one of those plastic accordian-fold wallet photo holders for swatches and favorite pattern yardage requirements. Look at it every time you make a fabric or accessory purchase and slap your hands if it doesn't fit into the "grand scheme of things". See illustration on previous page.

How to Make a Blazer in 8 Hours!

Pati is a super speedy seamstress who can make a blazer in 8 hours — but Susan (who usually sews at a snail's pace) can now make that 8 hour blazer too. Here are some secrets:

1. **Select a basic pattern** and plan to make it several times in different fabrics — each time you repeat a pattern it goes together faster and more easily.

2. Look for these **pattern features that are fast:**
   - patch pockets instead of welt
   - no back or sleeve vent (or stitch existing ones closed)
   - lining (faster than finishing seams in an unlined garment)
   - pattern must include a lining pattern
   - "Easy" patterns can be deceptive. They claim to be easy because there are fewer pattern pieces which means fewer seams, but . . . more darts. We feel that sewing and pressing darts is **not necessarily faster** and if you have fitting problems, the more seams you have to work with the easier to fit.

3. **Use no-fail, easy-to-tailor fabrics** (see page 16 for details). Look for these in order of speed:
   - textured double knit (fastest)
   - medium weight textured wools or wool blends (like tweed)
   - linen and linen-like fabrics

   Be sure to avoid (for an 8-hour blazer!):
   - velvets (harder to sew and take forever to press)
   - tightly woven permanent press fabrics (tend to pucker and are hard to ease)
   - plaids of any type (look great but take longer to cut and match)

4. **Use fastest methods:**
   - fusible interfacing fused directly to fabric (see page 70)
   - machine buttonholes (see page 108)
   - quick lining (see page 103)

Pattern Selection

1. Select a pattern with good lines for you. Some hints:

To make you look shorter and wider	To make you look taller and more slender

double breasted, wide lapels, square bottom	single breasted, medium width lapels, rounded bottom and deep "V" lapel (one or two button jacket)

short, boxy style	long jacket with princess seaming

If you're not sure about the best lines for you, try on ready-to-wear or analyze the lines of your favorite clothes.

Remember, almost any style or length jacket will add height and be slenderizing if the jacket and pants or skirt are in the same color fabric.

NOTE: ALWAYS look at the line drawings on the pattern or in the pattern book as they will give you the true shape of the fashion.

2. Buy the right pattern size (see page 42).

3. Choose an attractive jacket length.

If the pants or skirt fit well, jacket length is not as crucial. As a general rule, jackets should be long enough to hide the derriere because if a jacket stops at the fullest part of the hip, it will emphasize hip width. Overall proportion must also be considered — a short person may look better in a shorter jacket. Before making a jacket, pin the pattern pieces together and try on with the finished pants or skirt. A full length mirror will give you your answers.

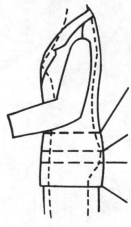

Short jackets — best with skirts. If worn with pants, pants must fit well and should be the same color.

Above fullest part of hip — OK for thin hips and short people.

Just below fullest part of hip — a "compromise length" when fashion decrees "short jackets". If jacket is to be worn with both pants and skirts, this is best length.

Well below fullest part of hip — hides hips best and is safest length for average to tall people.

Find a flattering length before you invest in a pattern by snoop shopping — try on different lengths in ready-to-wear jackets with both skirts and pants. When you find the lengths you like best, take your trusty purse tape measure out and measure the finished back length! Compare to the "finished back length" as printed on the pattern envelope.

4. Before you buy the pattern — check the pattern envelope. If the pattern does not have a lining pattern included, consider choosing another. It is harder to finish off all those seams so that they look pretty than to line a jacket. Cutting your own lining is possible, but time-consuming (see page 31).

5. Changes made in the roll line affect the gorge line and are difficult to deal with — select a pattern with a lapel, roll line, and number of buttons that you like. Life is too short to change a 3 button blazer into a 2 button blazer!

Choose a No-Fail Fabric

The No-Fail Fabric Chart was designed to show fast sewability at a glance. If you want an "8 Hour Blazer," be sure to choose a fabric from that column. These will fuse, sew and press quickly with professional results. Those in the "Not As Fast Fabrics" column require a bit more skill and often another tailoring method, but can still be sewn successfully.

A key to fast tailoring with fusibles is choosing a medium weight fabric with surface texture or design. A fabric with lumps or bumps (tweed), fuzz (flannel), texture (linen) or design (herringbone) will camouflage your interfacing and inner construction. Just like printed cotton hid mistakes on your 7th grade skirt, fabrics with surface interest will hide blazer errors!

If a fabric doesn't ease well, it will be harder to handle. You will be more likely to get puckers in your set-in sleeve, in seams, or at the lapel notch. Tightly woven fabrics, permanent press fabrics, and fabrics that contain a high percentage of non-absorbent fiber (nylon, polyester) don't ease well. A fabric like "Trigger®" which has all three of these characteristics will be difficult to tailor.

No-Fail Fabric Chart

8 Hour Blazer Fabrics*	Not As Fast Fabrics
Polyester or wool double knit	Corduroy
Wool tweed and wool flannel	Velvet
Linen and linen-like fabrics	Velveteen
Suit-weight silk	Seersucker
Wool blends	Heavy coating
Ultrasuede® brand fabric	Sportswear fabric
Textured or printed cotton	
Stretch woven polyester	
Wool gabardine	

*Listed in order of
sewing ease — easiest at top

Sewing and Shaping Tips for Tailoring Fabrics

Polyester double knit — Excellent for the 8 Hour Blazer and nearly goof-proof, knit is very durable, needs no seam finishing, and is the only blazer we would ever machine wash and dry (other than Ultrasuede®).

Wool double knit — Pendleton makes a lovely 18 oz. fabric that wears well and is easy to sew using any method.

Wool tweed (Anglo, Pendleton, JP Stevens) — The BEST, we mean THE BEST 8 Hour Blazer fabric you could ever use! It eases well so your sleeves will set in perfectly, and the texture hides inside construction. Some fusibles won't adhere well to lumpy surfaces, so always test fusibles on a sample to see which is best. Custom method is also suitable.

Wool flannel (Anglo, Pendleton, JP Stevens) — If you use a flannel, use a good one — a medium to heavy weight 100% wool is the easiest to tailor. Anglo makes a wonderful wool flannel called "Aristoc" that is worth every penny. Flannel is truly an 8 Hour Blazer fabric. Lightweight flannels need underlining for wrinkle resistance. Custom method is also suitable.

Linen — Moygashel's "Pembroke" (suitweight 100% linen) is one of our favorites and is one of the best 8 Hour Blazer fabrics. It is almost as easy to tailor as wool tweed. An added plus: fusing minimizes wrinkling. Use a lightweight fusible on the upper collar and front facing for added body. Always line or underline skirt and pant coordinates to control wrinkling.

Linen-like fabrics — These come in all weights from the heavier rayon/polyester blends like 60" wide "Icebound" or 100% fibo-rayon "Moymacrae" from Moygashel, to lightweights. The heavier, loosely woven fabrics are far easier to tailor than the lighter weight, tightly woven, permanent press blends. All methods are suitable, but the 8 Hour Blazer techniques are perfect for the heavier weights. Underlining is a way to add body to lightweight linen-like fabrics.

Suit-weight silk — Any method is suitable for this fabric. Many will lose body after cleaning, so use slightly heavier weight interfacings to compensate. Fusibles will add stability and wrinkle resistance. Use a lightweight fusible on upper collar and facings for added body, in addition to front and under collar interfacings. Underlining will also add body and stability.

Wool blends ("H$_2$O" by JP Stevens) — These fabrics are less expensive and often a little looser in weave and lighter in weight than 100% wools. Polyester and nylon are the common blending fibers. If blends are at least 50% wool they will still ease satisfactorily and be easy to sew for a cost-cutting 8 Hour Blazer. Wool blends are great for children's clothing as many are machine washable. If fabric needs more body, use a tailoring method with an underlining.

Ultrasuede® brand fabric (Skinner) — Definitely an 8 Hour Blazer fabric, but requires special sewing techniques. (See **Sewing Skinner® Ultrasuede® Fabric** by Pati Palmer and Susan Pletsch page 128).

Textured or printed cotton (denim, chino, poplin, madras) If stiff and tightly woven, they will be hard to tailor because they will resist easing. Woven or knit fusibles may leave a smoother surface on these fabrics. Prints hide sewing and pressing problems.

Stretch woven polyester (Burlington, Logantex, Skinner) One of the most widely distributed is Burlington's "Suraline," a gabardine. These fabrics are a good investment for year-round dressing and always look crisp and fresh. Any method can be used. If you fuse to the fabric, test first. Woven or knit fusibles may leave a smoother surface.

Wool gabardine (Anglo, Pendleton, JP Stevens, B.Black) Wool gabardine is made from long wool fibers that are highly twisted. It is tightly woven, has a smooth surface, and is available in medium and lightweights. Because of its smooth surface, gabardine shows press marks easily and requires careful pressing to avoid an overworked appearance. It is possible to use fusibles with wool gabardine, but always do a test sample to make sure a ridge doesn't show on the right side, or choose a pattern with a front dart or narrow front panel and camouflage interfacing edge by fusing to dart or seam. Avoid using a fusible on the back. Woven or knit fusibles may leave a smoother surface on these fabrics. Any tailoring method is suitable.

Corduroy — Some are 100% cotton and some are blended with polyester. All corduroys seem to shrink quite a bit, so we recommend machine washing and drying to preshrink if you plan to use a fusible interfacing — even if you plan to dry clean the finished garment. Also preshrink woven and knit fusibles (see page 41). Be sure to read your interfacing instructions. For example, you will find Pel-Aire and Tailor's Touch are recommended for corduroys, fine to medium wale corduroys will fuse better than wide wale, and fusibles should be cut on the crosswise grain. If piecing is needed when cutting crossgrain, piece at an inconspicuous point. Butt or slightly overlap lightweight fusibles. Medium weight fusibles should be pinked and then interlocking pinked edges butted together. Make a test sample to see which fusibles you like best.

Velvet — Velvets have a deeper, more erect pile than velveteens. True velvets are made of rayon or rayon/acetate while velveteens are made of cotton. The pile on velvet is fragile and heat sensitive. Fusing flattens the pile and leaves iron imprints. Any of the other tailoring methods would be better. We prefer simple, collarless jackets for velvet using modified custom or underlined shaping methods.

Velveteen — Velveteen has a less dense, less erect pile than velvet. If you fuse to it, you will flatten the pile and detract from its beauty. Any of the other tailoring methods work well. Some lightweight velveteens need to be underlined for more body.

Washable Velvet ("Matinee" from JB Martin) — This fabric is made on a velvet system giving it a deep, thick pile, but it is a blend of 65% cotton and 35% rayon, making it more heat tolerant. We have successfully fused to Matinee and have found it to wear better than velvet — you won't get shiny elbows or seat as with true velvet. "Street Velvet" (by JB Martin) is 100% cotton and has the same virtues, but has less sheen than Matinee. Use fusibles on the crossgrain. Preshrink woven and knit fusibles. Not all fusibles adhere well as these fabrics have soil release or silicone finishes that resist some fusing agents, so make a test sample. Custom and modified cutsom methods work well also. Amazingly, both fabrics are really machine washable!

Seersucker — If you want to use a fusible, use the "Easier" method and fuse to the underlining. Fusing directly to seersucker flattens the puckers you just paid for!

Heavy coatings ("Mazerak" or "Primosa" by Anglo or Pendleton's "Regency Fleece" — You may use the easiest method, but test interfacings to find one that adheres best to fuzzy surfaces. Due to the bulk of coatings, custom method may be the easiest and least bulky. Trim enclosed seams very close to stitching line and bevel to eliminate bulk (see page 53).

Sportswear fabrics ("Trigger" by Burlington/Klopman and "Kettle-cloth" by Concord) — These fabrics are tightly woven, lightweight and generally have a permanent press finish. Even though they are easy to care for, they are difficult to tailor and are not recommended for a first project.

The Critical Issue — Shaping Fabrics

The shape in a tailored garment is really important. We use much more subtle shaping and easier methods than in years past, but the need for support for your fashion fabric hasn't changed.

Remember that tailoring is different:

1.   Tailored garments receive greater strain due to more frequent wear.
2.   **When in doubt** — use a shaping fabric. Your clothing will look better and wear longer. No matter what you choose, the garment will look better and wear longer than if you used nothing.

Here are the layers as they relate to tailoring in order of application:

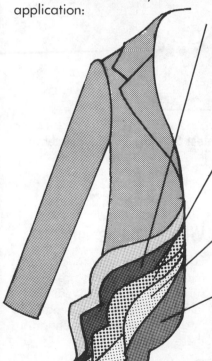

Underlining — Provides shape, body and support to large areas of a garment; for example, the body of a coat would be underlined, the collar interfaced. An underlining can also be a "cheat layer" to hold markings, make hems invisible, a place to tack interfacings and facings.

Interfacing — A generally firm fabric that is used to provide shape, body and support in small areas (edges and details) in a garment.

Interlining — A lofty layer of fabric stitched inside a garment to provide added warmth.

Lining — Fabric cut from separate pattern pieces that is assembled and then stitched inside the garment to cover the inside construction and to allow the garment to slide on and off easily.

Underlining

Choose underlining fabric by the amount of body needed to create the look you want from your fashion fabric. As fashion changes from shaped to softer silhouettes you may still want to use an underlining — it will make light colored fabric opaque, and will allow you to use speed techniques (like fusing) on fabrics that otherwise would not accept them.

How to Underline:

Basting an underlining in place is tedious and not always accurate. There is too much chance for the underlining to slip while sewing. **What is the answer?** SOBO GLUE! Sobo is a liquid fabric glue that dries fairly clear and soft. It can be found in most sewing and notion departments.

Underlining is simple — if you glue with Sobo!

1.   Place your fabric on a flat padded pressing surface. Steam press all the wrinkles out.

2.   Place your underlining on top and steam press the two together. This removes wrinkles and any possible shrinkage. Lift underlining and dot Sobo glue on fashion fabric close to the edge in **seam allowances**. Pat the two layers together. Allow 5 minutes to dry.

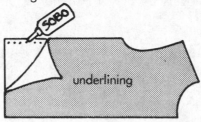

3.   For more underlining information, including the "Glue and Fold" technique, see **Mother Pletsch's Painless Sewing**, by Pati Palmer and Susan Pletsch.

Interfacing

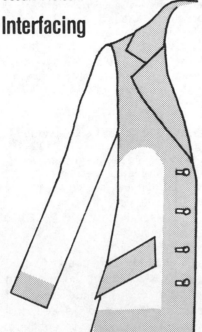

Where to Interface

Edges — (armhole, neck, front, hem) because edges are subject to excessive wear and interfacings provide strength, body, and stretch-prevention in these areas.

Details — (collar, cuff, pocket, band) because the fashion details of a garment should be a positive fashion statement — a firmly shaped collar, a crisply tailored belt, and pockets that won't droop.

How to Choose a Stitchable Interfacing:

Make a sandwich of your interfacing placed between two layers of the fashion fabric — this simulates the garment layers best. Feel them:

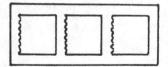

1. The interfacing should compliment the fashion fabric, not overpower it.
2. Try draping the two layers to resemble the place where they will be used. For example, fold them around your wrist to resemble a cuff.
3. The two fabrics should be care-compatible.

How to Choose a Fusible Interfacing

To decide exactly the right fusible interfacing for your fabric, you should make a **test sample**, since fusibles change in feel after fusing. Oooops — can't very well take the iron to the fabric store to test, can you? So bring the fabric store home — it's a good idea to buy 3 yards of several of those listed on page 24. (You'll save time on future sewing too.) After cutting out your blazer, fuse a test sample of several different interfacings (both wovens and non-wovens) to scraps of fabric.

1. Cut one side of the interfacing with pinking shears to see if this makes the edge blend into the fabric better. Fuse.
2. Now check your test sample for:

- Outside appearance — is there any color change or a ridge left from the cut edge of interfacing?
- Feel — do the interfacing and fashion fabric **feel good together**?
- Washability — toss the test sample into the washer/dryer to check the after appearance if you plan to wash the garment.

How to Fuse

Read and follow the manufacturer's instructions first. If unavailable then use these general instructions.

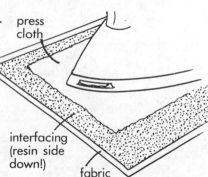

1. Preheat iron, set on "WOOL". Use steam.
2. Warm your fashion fabric by steam pressing.
3. Place your preshrunk interfacing (see page 41) resin side down on fabric.

4.   Steam baste in place by lightly touching your iron point to the interfacing in several spots.

5.   Use a damp press cloth, even if you use a steam iron, since more moisture gives a more even fuse.

6.   Fuse for 10 - 15 seconds per iron section without sliding the iron, and using two-handed pressure. Be sure to fuse for the full count or the fusible will be underfused and will eventually separate from the fabric.

7.   Be patient! Always allow fused pieces to cool before moving them.

NOTE: Use a minimum of 10 seconds to fuse any fabric. The heavier the fabric, the more seconds you should use. Susan uses the MISSISSIPPI trick. Count "One Mississippi", "Two Mississippi", etc. You will then be sure to count 10 full seconds.

Interfacing/Underlining Weight Chart for Tailored Garments

	Stitchable Interfacing	Fusible Interfacing	Underlining

LIGHT WEIGHT	W Armo Press Firm
	N Sheer Sew-In (Stacy)
	N Sheer weight Sew-In
	   Pellon #905
	W Veriform Durable
	   Press (Stacy)
		K Easy-Knit (Stacy)
		N Feather weight
		    fusible Pellon #911FF
		N Lightweight Easy-
		    Shaper (Stacy)
		W Shape-Flex All-
		    Purpose (Stacy)
		N Sof-Shape Pellon
		    #880F
		N So Sheer (Armo)
		WI Whisper Weft
		    (Armo)
			W Armo Press Soft
			   (stitchable)
			W Poly SiBonne Plus
			   (stitchable)
			W Poly-cotton batiste
			   (stitchable)
			W Silk organza
			   (stitchable)

MEDIUM	W Acro (Armo)
	N Add-Shape Medium-
	   lite (Stacy)
	W Lady Hymo (B.Black)
		WI Armo Weft
		N Pel-Aire #881F
		    (Pellon)
		WI Suit Shape (Stacy)
		N Suitweight Easy-
		    Shaper (Stacy)
		N Tailor's Touch (Stacy)
			W Armo Press Firm
			   (stitchable)
			K Easy-Knit (Stacy)
			   (fusible)
			W Veriform Durable
			   Press (Stacy)
			   (stitchable)

HEAVY	W Armo P-1/Fino II
	W Armo P26 Red Edge
	W Hair Canvas #77
	   (Stacy)
	W Wool Hymo
	   (B.Black)
		W Fusible Acro (Armo)	Use the medium weights above or use a medium weight hair canvas

Key: **W** - Woven   **WI** - Weft insertion
      N - Nonwoven   **K** - Knit

Answers to Common Questions About Fusibles

Which fusibles work best with which fabrics? The only absolute answer is a test sample. Woven fusibles generally produce the smoothest look on flat fabrics — gabardine, poplin, etc. Non-woven fusibles generally fuse best to textured fabrics. If your fabric is lumpy or fuzzy, interfacings with fusing agents applied in dot form will often adhere better.

How do I keep buttonholes from stretching when I use a fusible with crosswise give? Stabilize the buttonhole area with a piece of organdy, organza, or sheer no-stretch interfacing.

What is a "weft insertion" interfacing? Weft insertion interfacings (Armo Weft, Whisper Weft, and Suit Shape) are knits with a woven-in crosswise yarn. These interfacings have the drapability of a knit, the crosswise stability of a woven, and can produce a bias direction like a woven.

Why does every interfacing have different instructions for fusing? Each product is different and each manufacturer writes instructions after thoroughly testing to find out how to get the best fuse. It is even important to read the instructions when you buy a new piece of the same brand as manufacturers are constantly improving fusibles which can change the fusing instructions.

Why would I want to use more than one type of interfacing in the same jacket? Combinations of interfacings provide versatility — your fabric may function best with a medium weight fusible in the front and collar, a lighter weight fusible on the pockets, hems, upper collar and facings, and a stitchable interfacing in the back. Another reason to have an "interfacing store" at home!

Can I fuse to napped fabrics like corduroy? Yes, with some cautions. See page 18 for specific directions. A test sample here is very important.

Does fusing give the same good results as hand stitches in custom tailoring? In custom tailoring, lapels and collars are rolled into shape while stitching to make them permanent.

With fusibles, they are fused flat then reheated into the rolled shape with heat and steam. When they cool in that rolled position, the shape is permanent. The fusing agent is thermoplastic — meaning it can be heat-set into a permanent shape.

Do I need to preshrink interfacings? See page 41 for details. We feel that preshrinking is an "all or nothing" matter — preshrink everything, or preshrink nothing and hope all pieces shrink at the same rate. Preshrinking one piece but not others means instant incompatibility.

Why do I get "bubbles" with fusing? There are two different types of bubbles that can occur. Bubbles in your fashion fabric indicate that your fusible has shrunk more than your fashion fabric. Bubbles on the interfacing side indicate the opposite — your fashion fabric has shrunk more than the interfacing causing puckers or bubbles to appear.

To solve the problem, remember our "all or nothing" philosophy. When you preshrink all pieces you are assuring yourself that all ingredients will fuse without bubbles and wash or dry clean without shrinking. If you preshrink nothing, you have to trust that all ingredients indeed will shrink at the maximum allowable rate for a product to be called "preshrunk", which is 1½%.

Why don't the interfacing manufacturers tell me to preshrink my fusibles? These manufacturers have already put their product through strict shrinking processes, and have arrived at a maximum shrinkage percentage of no more than 1½%, which is a very small amount. So they feel your interfacing should perform satisfactorily. We feel that your interfacing should have a 0% shrinkage, which cannot physically be done by a manufacturer. If YOU preshrink a piece of interfacing in YOUR humidity, AFTER it has been cut from the bolt and allowed to relax, using our recommended preshrinking methods (see page 41) then you have done what would be impossible for the manufacturer to do.

But if I preshrink my fusible in hot water, won't it fuse to itself? Fusibles are activated by temperatures of 300° and up. Hot tap water is never hot enough to soften the fusible resin. Even the clothes dryer is not hot enough to loosen a well fused interfacing in a finished garment.

What causes those ugly "polka dots" in fused areas on the right side of the fabric that appear after laundering? "Strike through" is caused by using the wrong fusible on the fabric, and happens more with sheer to light weight fabrics than with tailoring weights. Some fusible dots will be simply too thick for your fabric and will creep through in laundering to cause that speckled effect. Choosing a different type of fusible solves the problem.

Cut the Best Interfacing Shape

If your pattern does not include interfacing pattern pieces, or if they are not similar in shape to these, you will want to cut your own pattern pieces. Draw a line with a soft tip pen on pattern pieces as shown. Cut.

Front: You will have the best shaping, best wear, and least wrinkling when the interfacing covers the bustline and extends to the armhole edge. Notice the curved edge of the interfacing — this helps it blend in better than a straighter line.

Front: Stitchable

Front: Fusible
Extend interfacing to dart stitching line to cushion interfacing cut edge.

Back: Stitchable or Fusible

Side Panel: Stitchable or Fusible
(You will get less wrinkling under the arm if it is interfaced.)

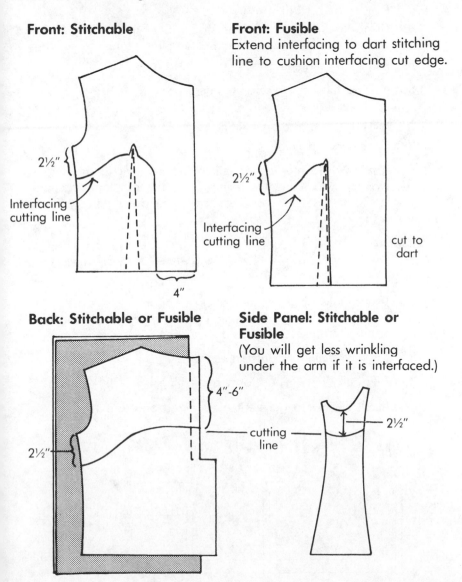

Interlining

An interlining is the layer that adds extra warmth to a coat or jacket. These fabrics should add warmth but not weight, so look for a lightweight but lofty fabric. Some suggestions:

1. Armo Wool — a loosely woven wool — dry clean only.
2. Pellon Polyester Fleece or Thermolam — washable non-woven fleece.
3. Outing flannel — a washable cotton or cotton/polyester flannel (be sure to preshrink!).
4. Armo-Rite or Canvas Unlimited (Stacy) — lofty woven washable polyester/rayon lambs wool-like fabric.
5. Polyester needlepunch.

Some lining fabrics are self-interlined:
1. Pre-quilted fabrics
2. Millium — an insulated lining
3. Fleece-backed lining

The easiest way to interline is to stitch the interlining to the lining — in other words, to underline the lining! Since the interlining occupies some of the inside ease, it is usually placed in the body of the garment but not in the sleeves.

To interline:

1. Cut interlining from lining pattern pieces, omitting back pleat and hem.

2. Temporarily baste center back pleat in lining closed. Pin corresponding lining/interlining pieces together and machine baste all edges ½" from edge.

3. Assemble lining as pattern suggests.

4. Trim bulky interlining close to stitching line.

5. Stitch lining into garment as directed on page 101.

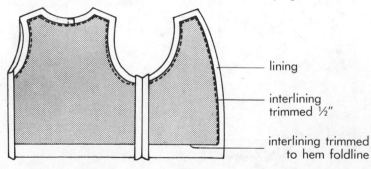

lining

interlining trimmed ½"

interlining trimmed to hem foldline

Lining

The finishing touch — the lining layer — can be as gorgeous or functional as you want it to be. A lining should cover the inside construction, so an opaque fabric is important; a slick fabric makes putting on and taking off the garment easier; a lining fabric should be as long-wearing as the fashion fabric (relining a jacket or coat is NOT FUN!) See page 101 for lining methods.

For functional purposes, we really like polyester linings — they wear forever, are easy to handle, and maintain their shape well. Some suggestions:

1. Ciao — polyester crepe by Armo

2. Ala Creme, Noblese, Palazzio — elegant polyester wovens from Skinner

3. Sen-Sensual from Skinner or Casheen by Logantex — both are polyester tissue faille

But for summer comfort we often choose rayon, acetate, or rayon/acetate blends. These fabrics are not quite as durable or as washable, but they have the advantage of being made of fibers that breathe. These often are produced with a small woven design or imprinted with a designer's logo. How about a Bill Blass jacket with Bill's own logo on the lining!

But for fun — forget about trying to match that fashion fabric and find a contrasting lining that will add pzazz! Prints are super (make matching shirt or soft dress for an elegant costume). If wearing a print lined jacket over a different print dress offends you, look for some of the inoffensive and insignificant prints that really blend well with anything. Stripes, dots, checks, and small two-color prints are very versatile. Even in conservative menswear, linings are often loud but gorgeous — we saw a black gabardine Pierre Cardin business suit with a smashing RED PLAID lining!

NOTE: Susan has a beautiful silk scarf that she plans to recycle soon into a jacket lining. The scarf is large enough to line the jacket body and she will find a coordinating solid fabric for the sleeves.

Cutting a Lining With a Pattern

Linings in coats and jackets need a pleat for wiggle room and to keep the sleeves from tearing out with stress. If your pattern does not have a pleat, follow the method below:

1. Place lining back pattern on fold, slanting pattern so 1" is added at neckline tapering to nothing at bottom. Cut.

2. Stitch down 1½" to anchor pleat at neckline.

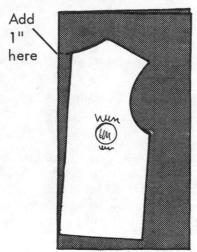

Add 1" here

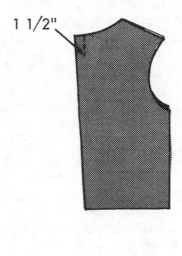

1 1/2"

If you are using the Quick Lining method (see page 103) cut the underarm of the bodice and sleeve ¼" higher to allow lining to go up and over the sleeve underarm seam.

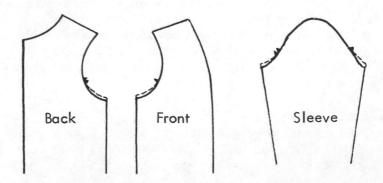

Back   Front   Sleeve

See page 106 for more on cutting a lining for a vented jacket.

Cutting a Lining Without a Pattern

When your pattern has no lining pattern pieces, but your fabric needs a lining, cut one following these instructions.

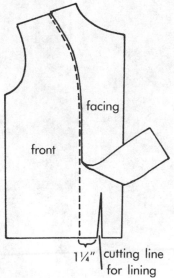

Front — Place facing pattern piece on jacket pattern piece, mark facing edge with dotted line. Measure 1¼" from edge of facing as shown, for cutting line for lining.

Back — Use back pattern piece. Allow a pleat as on page 30. Eliminate back facing from top of lining using same method as above for eliminating front facing.

Sleeve — Cut same as garment sleeve eliminating vent.

Easy Seam Finishes for an "Unlined" Jacket

Ravelly seams are unattractive. Make the inside of your jacket pretty using one of these easy finishes as you sew the seams.

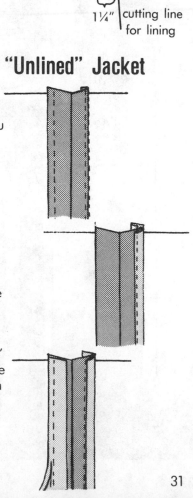

Turn and stitch — Stitch ¼" from raw edge. Turn edge of seam allowance under on that stitching line and edge stitch.

Bind edges with double-fold ¼" bias binding, or Seams Great or Seams Saver, or pre-folded lace. Slip over seam edge and topstitch in place. Use a contrasting color if you can't get a perfect match.

Hong Kong seam finish — Sew a 1" wide bias strip of lining fabric to edge of seam, right sides together, ¼" from edge. Trim to ⅛". Turn lining to wrong side and topstitch in well of seam from top side to catch in place. Trim.

Sometimes a Great Notion

Have these sewing aids on hand at all times — especially for tailoring! See referenced pages for more about "how to use".

GADGET	USE	PAGE
Cutting and Marking Aids		
1. Pins (long, large head)	Pins thick fabrics easily	52
2. Sewing gauge (6" ruler)	Marks hems & buttonholes	97, 108
3. Sharp shears (long, bent handle)	Smooth, even cutting	50
4. Pinking shears	Cutting fusible interfacings, seam finishing	70
5. Embroidery scissors or tailor points (Gingher)	Ripping/clipping/ snipping/trimming	53, 96
6. Tracing wheel (smooth-edged) and washable tracing paper (Dritz)	Speedy marking	52
7. Water soluble marker (Collins, Dritz)	Easily removed marking	49, 52
8. Tailor's chalk with holder (Dritz, Singer)	Easily removed marking	49, 52
Sewing Aids		
1. Topstitching tape (Collins)	Premarked sewing tape for accurate topstitching	122
2. Sobo Glue	Liquid glue for glue-basting underlining and interfacing	22,61,64, 66,69
3. Baste & Sew Glue Stik™ (Collins, Dritz)	Glue stick for glue-basting	64,65,68
4. Singer "Yellow Band" sewing machine needles	Prevents skipped stitches	122
5. Point turner/creaser	Turns corners right side out	96
6. Fray Check (Dritz, Singer)	Prevents raveling on seam edges	122
7. Seams Great or Seams Saver (Stacy)	Nylon tricot seam binding	31

Now Organize These Gadgets:

1.   Hang a mug rack on the wall — the handiest way we have found to store all "grab-for" items. Tie a pretty ribbon loop on items that don't want to hang.

2.   Find a small chest of drawers to put next to the machine for storing small supplies and pressing equipment.

3.   Keep an organizer tray on your machine for small items that won't hang on the mug rack.

4.   Hang a bulletin board above the machine to hold pattern pieces, guide sheets, hand needles.

5.   Pin a paper lunch bag on the ironing board and tape one to the machine for scraps and threads — we hate to pick up threads!

NOTE — A FREE organizer — if you sew next to a window with a curtain, pin your pattern directions to the curtain so they are easy to find and follow.

Learn to Press
Pressing Equipment

Don't even consider making a tailored garment unless you have (or are willing to purchase) some basic pressing equipment. The **absolute essentials** are:

1. **Seam roll** — a sausage-shaped gadget used to press open flat seams and cylinders like sleeves and pant legs. The seam allowances fall over the edge of the roll and allow your iron to touch only the stitching line itself.

2. **Pressing ham** (tailor's ham) — a ham-shaped surface ideal for pressing curved and shaped areas, helps give "people shape" to flat fabric.

3. **Point presser/clapper** — a wooden combination tool used to press open seams and points, and to flatten a seam by holding heat and steam in a fabric. Often used with a seam roll or ham.

4. **Steam iron** — look for one with lots of holes. We like the "shot-of-steam" types with an extra button to push for a jet of steam that will press even the most stubborn fabric.

There are some fantastic pressing aids that we love for tailoring and hope you will try. But these are **optional**.

1. **June Tailor's Tailor Board** — the most versatile pressing tool. This marvelous thing has several "can't live without" surfaces. The long curved edge is perfect for pressing open a curved collar seam, or blazer front. Small curve just fits rounded collars or cuffs, and the point presser end is the best way to press into collar points. Works best with optional padded cover on top surface.

2. **Press Mitt** — Have you ever wanted to press something on a hanger but didn't know how? Just slip your hand into the press mitt and use your protected and shaped "hand" as your ironing board in the air.

3. **See-through press cloths** — a sheer press cloth that allows you to see what you're pressing and still protect the fabric.

4. **June Tailor Velvaboard** — a super item! It holds steam in a unique bristled pad, then reflects it back into napped fabrics to steam press without flattening nap.

> **NOTE:** Fingers are a FREE pressing tool! You can slightly finger press a seam or dart in the right direction BEFORE permanently pressing with the iron or pounding block.

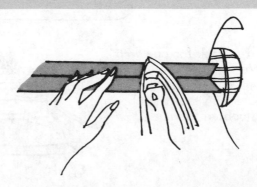

Press As You Sew

"Press as you sew" has been preached for years, but nowhere is it quite as important as in tailoring. Please don't think you can ignore pressing and pay your cleaners to press after you've finished. Cleaners can often do a nice **final press** — but how can they possibly get inside your jacket after it's completed? So move the ironing board next to your sewing machine, adjust the board to machine table height, and then sew, swivel, press, sew, swivel, press.

1. Test press a scrap of fabric first.

2. Press with an "up and down" motion of the iron whenever possible, otherwise slide iron along seam in ONE direction in order to make a smooth seam.

3. Use lots of steam.

4. Press on the wrong side. Use a press cloth if fabric is heat-sensitive.

How to Press: A Seam

1. Press seam as it was stitched to remove any puckers, and to blend stitches.

2. Place seam over seam roll. Saturate with steam by holding iron ⅛" above fabric surface.

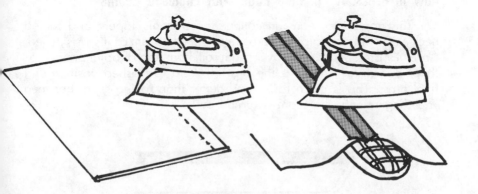

3. Place point presser/clapper on top of seam and apply light pressure. Hold clapper on seam until fabric is cool. This prevents warm fabric from stretching out of shape, and flattens seam better than the iron can do.

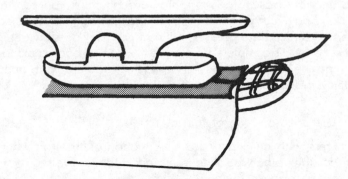

4. Top-pressing in our book is fine. Most pressing should be done from the inside to prevent possible shine, but do top-press when construction pressing hasn't quite done the trick. Saturate with steam, then fingerpress or gently flatten with clapper.

NOTE: Pressing takes **PATIENCE**!! Too-speedy pressing can create an overpressed, shiny, "I'm old and worn" look in a new garment. Synthetic fabrics will overpress more quickly than natural fabrics because the fibers are more heat-sensitive, so use a very light touch with these.

How to Press: A Finished Edge with Enclosed Seams

This applies to seams in collars, faced fronts, lapels, and curved necklines. Trim and clip where necessary. Press seam as it was stitched. Carefully press seam open over seam roll, ham, top of point presser, or tailor board, (whichever is the best fit). Fold to finished position and final press. This is much faster and better than rolling seam between your fingers until the seam is turned out!

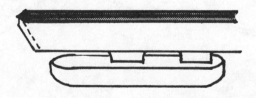

How to Press: A Dart

Press dart as it was stitched to flatten fold line and to blend stitches together. Place the dart over the appropriate curve of the ham and tuck paper under fold to prevent an indentation from showing on the right side. Steam. Flatten with point presser/clapper.

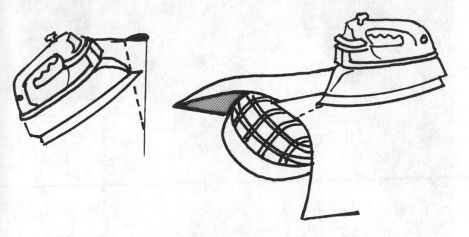

NOTE: The ham has many curves on it — one for every part of your body. Bust darts go over the very round curve at edge of ham, skirt darts over a flatter curve on top surface of ham.

Hints for Darts:

1. If dart is bulky, clip open and put strips of paper under edges to prevent press marks on right side. Press.

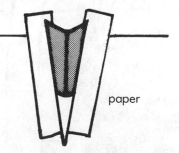

paper

2. Vertical darts are pressed toward the center for consistency.

3. Horizontal darts may be pressed down or up. We think pressing darts up gives a smoother, higher-busted younger look.

NOTE: Press lightly — If it isn't flat enough at first then lightly press again. And again. And again. Much better than too much the first time for a shiny, old look.

Preshrink!

Fashion Fabric

If you plan to:

1.   Wash your tailored garment, preshrink in washer and dryer with detergent and same water temperature you plan to use when laundering.

2.   Dry clean your garment by the clean and press method, take your fabric to the drycleaners and have them pre-shrink it for you. This heavy steaming process will remove potential shrinkage caused by pressing and fusing.

3.   Use the "clean only" drycleaning method at a bulk cleaners, simply pre-steam your fabric on your cutting board (cover with a sheet if it is not a padded board). This will eliminate the possible shrinkage from pressing as you sew. Steam evenly and move the iron with the grain across the fabric. Do not move iron in bias direction.

Interfacings:

Hair canvas should be dampened and pressed until dry.

Preshrink woven fusibles and fusible knits by the dunk method:

1.   Fold into a tidy square and place in basin of **hot** water for 10 minutes.

2.   Roll in towel to remove excess water, hang over towel bar to dry.

Preshrink nonwoven fusibles by the steam shrink process:

1.   Warm fashion fabric by pressing with steam to remove wrinkles and remaining shrinkage.

2.   Place interfacing on fabric (resin side down).

3.   Hold iron 1"-2" above interfacing and steam for 5 seconds. (A "Shot-of-Steam" type iron is a great help — it does a better and faster job.)

4.   Fuse together.

Linings:

Preshrink washable linings in washer and dryer. Steam press dry cleanable linings. Preshrink hand washable linings by the dunk method above.

Make Sure It Will Fit

Pattern Size

Buy the same size you would normally buy, because pattern companies automatically build in the extra ease needed for a coat or jacket to be worn over other clothes. **Don't buy a larger pattern size** for a heavy coating. Simply add "in-case" seams ("in-case" you need them!). Cut 1" seam allowances rather than ⅝" at shoulders, armholes, and sides of **both** the front and back pattern pieces. Then if the fabric takes up extra room as it goes around your body, you can let the seams out.

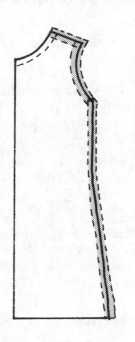

Ease

Try on a jacket you currently have in your wardrobe to see how much ease you are accustomed to.

"Quick Pinch Test": Pinch the body and sleeve of a jacket to check the ease in a garment. If you pinch 2", that means that your jacket has 4" of ease at that spot. (You are pinching a double thickness of fabric.) Be sure you are pinching **only** one side, pulling all the fabric to that side.

Built-in Ease Chart

	Bust	Hip	Sleeve (upper arm)	Back*
Unlined Jacket	3-4"	3-4"	3-4"	1-1½"
Lined Jacket	3½-4½"	3½-4½"	3-4½"	1-1½"
COAT (simple body shape)	4-5"	4-5"	4-5½"	1-2"

*6" below neck, armhole to armhole (Reaching room!)

NOTE: See how the garment is shown on the pattern envelope. If a coat is shown worn over a jacket, then enough extra ease has been allowed for that purpose. If it is shown only over a lightweight dress, that is how it is meant to be worn and it will not have enough ease to be worn over anything bulkier. However, coats with lower and wider cut armholes, square armholes, or raglan sleeves can usually be worn over a blazer-type jacket.

Two Ways to Fit a Pattern

1. **Try the Pattern On** — (The easiest). Trim excess tissue away and press pattern with warm dry iron. Pin in the darts and pin front and back seam together with seam allowances pinned to the **outside**. Clip the armhole and neckline curve of the tissue pattern so it will lie flat. Try the pattern on over the same type of clothes you'll be wearing under the finished jacket. Pin the **pattern** center front and back to **your** center front and back — to your **clothes** that is! Slip in shoulder pad.

Tissue Fit Checkpoints

(Always work from the top down so you won't miss anything).

Shoulder seam — at center of shoulder.*

Shoulder width — ¼"-½" beyond pivot bone in shoulder. (Jacket is worn **over** other clothes.) (See page 99 for variations.)

Grain line — perpendicular to floor at center back and front.

Side seams — hang straight. If your hips are larger than pattern, unpin so that pattern may fall freely. If side seams swing toward front, you have a sway back.

Bust darts — point to bust, but end 1" from point of bust.

Armhole — fits smoothly. If the armhole gaps in the front, it means your bust is fuller than pattern; if the armhole gaps in the back, it means you have a rounded back.

Waist — should be at waist. (Waist is marked on pattern by dots at side seams.)

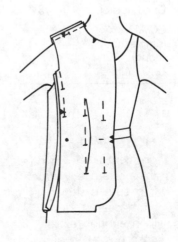

Length — Make sure hemline hits you at the most flattering part of your hip. This generally means below the fullest part of the derriere. (See page 14.)

Sleeve — Try the sleeve pattern on after first checking the above. Pin large dot at top of sleeve to shoulder and pin underarm seam in place. Width is checked by pinching pattern at upper arm across from under arm to see amount of ease. Length — hemline should hit middle of wrist bone (or ½" below it for a coat).

* Shoulder seams in some jackets angle toward the back as a design line. Check line drawing of jacket to see if shoulder is intentionally angled toward back.

2. **Flat Pattern Measure** — If in doubt after trying on the tissue pattern — double check with a tape measure. For example, if the side seams of the pattern won't come together, measure the pattern at the hip area and compare to your body hip measurement to see how much you actually need to add to the sides.

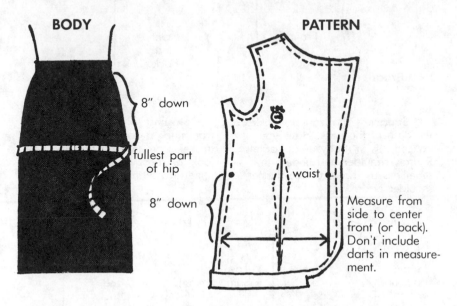

BODY   PATTERN

8" down

fullest part of hip

8" down

waist

Measure from side to center front (or back). Don't include darts in measurement.

If pattern front and back measure 20", (that is really 40" since you are cutting double), and your hip is 36" at the fullest part, then your pattern allows 4" ease which should be ample.

> **NOTE:** Always flat pattern measure in the exact same place you measured your body.

Special Tailoring Alterations

Alter a jacket in the same manner you would alter any other garment; however, the bulk of the fabric (in tailoring) often hides minor problems. (The following are problems you should **be sure** to correct.)

1. Shoulder Adjustments

Broad or narrow — Is the sleeve seam extending just past the shoulder pivot bone? If not, redraw seam line from notches up.

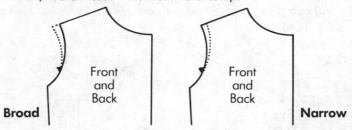

Broad

Front and Back

Front and Back

Narrow

Square — horizontal wrinkles at the base of the neck. Have you noticed this in ready made jackets? Redraw shoulder and underarm seamlines as shown or use thinner shoulder pads.

Sloping — diagonal wrinkles from neck to lower armhole. Use thicker shoulder pads (for the best look) or redraw shoulder and underarm seamlines as shown.

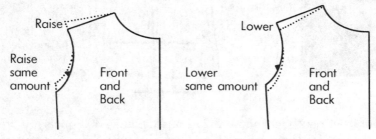

Raise

Raise same amount

Front and Back

Lower

Lower same amount

Front and Back

2. Dart Position

Bust darts should point toward the bust point (apex) and end 1" away from apex.

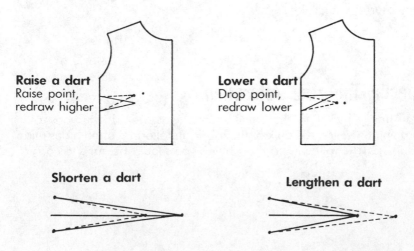

Raise a dart
Raise point, redraw higher

Lower a dart
Drop point, redraw lower

Shorten a dart

Lengthen a dart

3. Enlarge Bustline

Patterns are made for B bra cup size. A C cup should have no problem, but a D cup or larger should add extra room. If you have a diagonal wrinkle from armhole to bust or gaping front armhole you need to make this alteration.

> **NOTE:** This alteration is the same in a jacket with a side panel — the dart will still be in the front, but will be a bit shorter.

1. Find apex — Try pattern on and mark point of bust with a soft tip pen.

2. Draw line (A) on your pattern where you would like a dart.

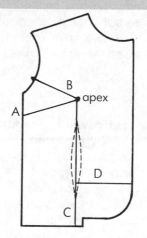

3. Draw line (B) from apex to armhole notch.

4. Draw line (C) vertically below apex to bottom of jacket (through center of dart if you have one).

5. Draw line (D) above front curve.

6. Cut on lines (C) and (B) to, but not through armhole. Cut on line (A) to, but not through apex. At arrow spread: ½" for C cup; ¾" for D cup; 1¼"-1½" for DD cup.

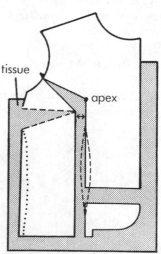

7. Cut (D) and drop until hems are even. Insert tissue and tape in place. Side opening becomes dart. Raise or lower dart if necessary. Take off from front side seam if now too full through waist or hip.

After you sew the horizontal bustline dart, your front and back side seams will again be the same length.

> **NOTE:** Three added bonuses: your armhole will no longer gap; you will have more width across the bust; you will have more length going over your larger bust and your jacket will no longer hike up at bottom in the front.

4. "Gaposis" of the roll line.

Simply shorten twill tape when sewing to pull in the roll line so it hugs your chest (see page 54). If it gaps a large amount, shorten roll line by taking a tuck in pattern. (Be sure to make this change on interfacing and facing also). This does not change the position of the roll line. It still begins and ends at the same points.

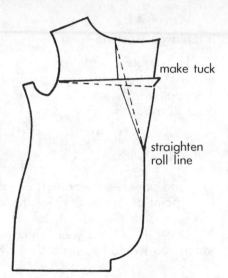

make tuck

straighten roll line

5. Extra width needed in the hip area.

Add equally to front, back and side panel, beginning at armhole. Divide amount you need to add (2") by the number of side seam allowances (4 on each side=8). Add that amount 2"÷8=¼") to each side as shown when you cut.

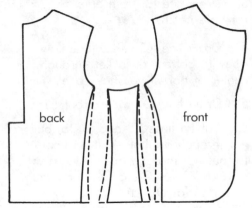

back

front

6. Sleeve too tight in upper arm.

Measure arm at underarm area. Alter sleeve as follows:

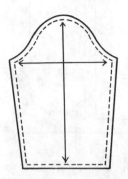

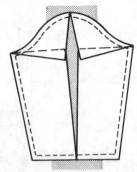

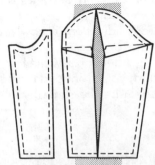

Measure pattern at underarm area.

To add, cut on grainlines as shown and spread desired amount.

Spread a 2 piece sleeve as shown above.

7. Sway back or erect back causes side seams to swing forward, center back to swing toward side and vent to spread open. Pin pattern to back. Take tuck until pattern center back hangs straight. (Tuck may be made higher or lower or even 2 small tucks). Straighten center back by drawing line connecting top and bottom.

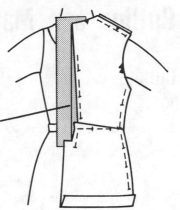

Fitting As You Sew

After you have completed the front and back, pin side and shoulder seams **wrong sides together** with pins on seam line. Pin up hem.

Try on **right side out** since right and left sides of body are different.

> **NOTE:** The neck must be staystitched so that it won't stretch (see page 61). If the fabric is stretchy or loosely woven, you should not hang the jacket on a hanger until the collar is stitched on.

You can adjust the ease around the body by pinning deeper or shallower side seams. You may also want to modify jacket for your figure by slightly tapering each side seam in ⅛"-¼" at the waist. This gives a slightly more slender look by creating an hourglass illusion.

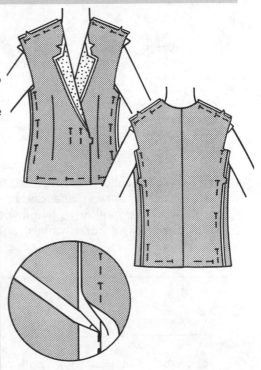

> **NOTE:** After you have made all your adjustments, mark new seam lines. Spread open seam allowances and mark at pins on wrong side of garment using tailors' chalk or water soluble marking pen.

Cutting and Marking are Related

Cutting

1. Lining (see page 30).

2. Interfacing (see page 27).

3. Fashion fabric — things to check for before cutting:

• Upper collar must be larger than under collar and facing must be larger than lapel (see page 55 for explanation of "turn-of-cloth"). The amount depends on the weight of your fabric. All patterns should allow at least ⅛". You may want to add more if your fabric is very heavy.

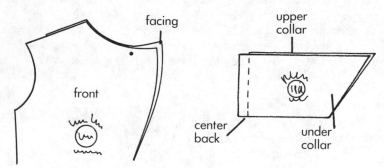

Lay jacket front pattern over facing pattern at lapel.

Lay upper collar pattern piece over under collar pattern piece.

• For a rolled collar that rolls smoothly, the under collar should be on the bias and cut in two pieces and have a center back seam. A one-piece all bias collar will have lengthwise grain (which is stronger) in opposite directions at collar points, and left and right may end up looking different.

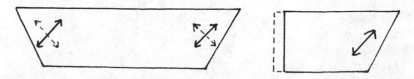

To correct: Cut pattern in half and add a center back seam allowance.

Marking

1. Snip Mark when cutting for speed and greater accuracy. Cut off notches and snip ¼" into edge on all pieces — fashion fabric, underlining, interfacing and lining. Snip mark all dots and matching points. Snip mark all the following:

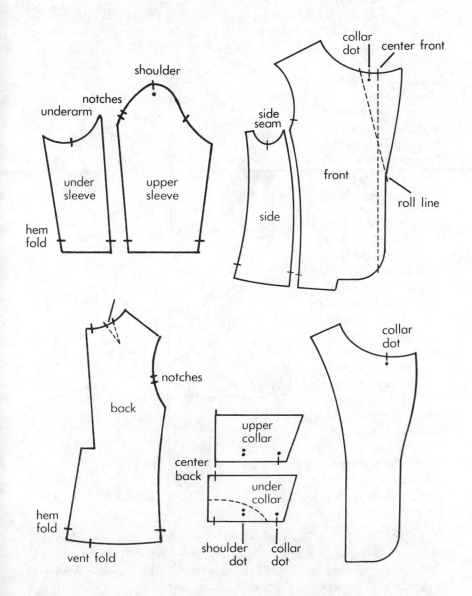

2. Additional markings
on underlining

Use a tracing wheel and washable tracing paper or water soluble marker to mark darts. It is not necessary to mark darts on fashion fabric.

on fashion fabric

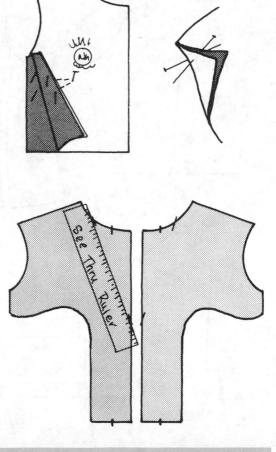

Try the tracing wheel. If it doesn't work, use the "pin-marking" method. Put pins through pattern dots. Remove pattern. Put pins in the bottom layer in the same place the pins came through. Now pin darts in place. Pins falling out? Mark the pin position with water soluble marker.

on interfacing

Mark buttonholes, roll line and center front using lead or chalk pencil and ruler. Lay left and right interfacing on the table facing each other. Place the ruler between snips and draw a line with a pencil. When applying interfacing to fabric, pencil marks should be on top.

See Thru Ruler

Tailoring What's and Why's

These are some of the techniques that universally apply to tailored garments and the reasons why they are used . . .

1. Eliminating Bulk

Why: There are usually more layers of fabric used in tailoring and often heavier than in a dress or skirt.

Interfacing — The interfacings in a tailored garment are generally heavier; therefore interfacing is not included in darts, neck, front, and underarm seams. Trim seams and darts away if your pattern has not done so. For stitchable interfacings: remove full ⅝" seam allowance. For fusibles: remove ½" of seam allowance, ⅛" is included in seam.

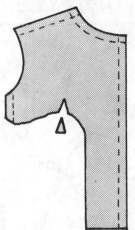 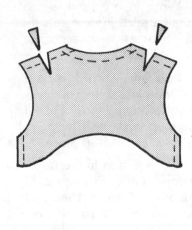

If your fabric is very bulky, you may also want to trim interfacing out of corners of a very pointed collar.

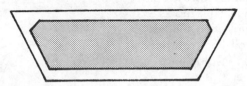

Enclosed seams — due to the extra bulk of fabric and extra layers of shaping fabrics used in tailoring, it is necessary to trim and grade or bevel seams.

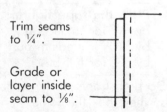

Trim seams to ¼".

Grade or layer inside seam to ⅛".

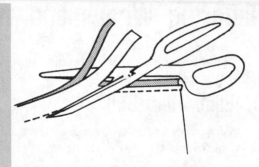

NOTE: You may trim and grade by "beveling." Simply slant scissors while trimming and one layer will automatically be narrower. Super on heavy coatings too — bevel seams one layer at a time.

Darts — usually slashed and pressed open to spread the bulk evenly. (See page 39).

2. Taping

Why: Tape is used to prevent stretch in garments that receive excessive wear such as a coat or jacket.

Roll line — which is on the bias. Tape keeps the roll line from stretching. Place ¼" twill tape (preshrunk) next to the roll line and fell stitch in place.

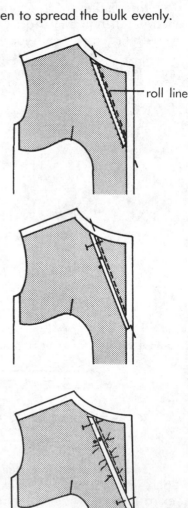

roll line

Go one step further and pull the tape tighter to prevent "gaposis" of the neckline and force the lapel to roll. Pin one end of tape next to roll line. Make a pencil mark on the tape and mark on the interfacing the appropriate distance away. Pull other end of tape until marks line up. Pin, distributing fullness equally along roll line from top to bottom. Stitch in place easing evenly onto tape.

> **PULL the tape tighter:**
> by ¼" for small bust
> by ⅜" for medium bust
> by ½" for full bust

Do both fronts at the same time so they look the same.

Front and neck edges — taping prevents stretch and eliminates bulk in seams by holding interfacing (with seam allowances trimmed away) in place (use ½" seam tape — preshrunk).

Clip tape and spread for inward curves like the neckline and clip tape and overlap on outward curves like the bottom of a jacket. Make sure uncut edge of tape is next to seam line.

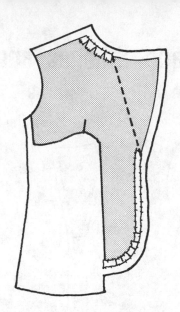

NOTE: If a fabric is stable or garment is not one you'll wear a lot, you may eliminate taping edges. Taping may be eliminated in the fusible method if the interfacing is included in seams.

3. Allowing for "Turn-of-cloth" — in lapel and collar

Why: It takes more fabric for the upper collar to roll over the under collar. Add to the outer edges of the upper collar if upper collar pattern piece is not already larger. (See page 50).

How much to add:
⅛" for light-medium weight fabric
¼" for medium-heavy weight fabric
⅜" for very heavy coatings

Also check lapel. Facing should be cut larger. See page 50 for how to cut larger if not allowed by pattern.

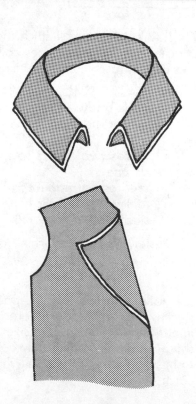

Hand Stitches and their Alternatives

in "Custom" Method

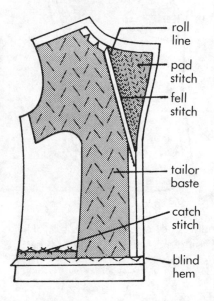

- roll line
- pad stitch
- fell stitch
- tailor baste
- catch stitch
- blind hem

in "Easiest" Method

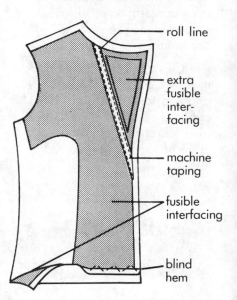

- roll line
- extra fusible inter-facing
- machine taping
- fusible interfacing
- blind hem

1. Pad stitch — small stitch that attaches interfacing to under collar and lapel. It accomplishes 3 things in one:

- **adds body** — the closer and smaller the stitches, the more body.
- **forces two layers to behave as one**
- **creates permanent roll** by folding layers over hand while stitching (see page 82).

Easier Ways: by machine or by fusing.

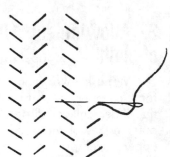

2. Tailor basting — large pad stitches used to hold large areas of interfacing in place. Use a size 10 sharp needle and catch only a fiber of fashion fabric so stitch won't show or catch only underlining.

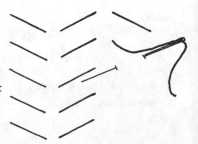

3. Fell stitch — a ⅜" long stitch used to hold tape tightly in place.

    Easier Way: May machine stitch tape in place. (See page 67).

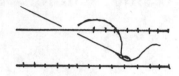

4. Catch stitch — a loose stitch used to catch edges of interfacing in place. Because it is loose, it will not ceate an interfacing ridge on the right side.

    Easier Way: May use a fusible interfacing.

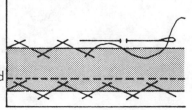

hem fold

5. Blind hem — a loose stitch done on inside of hem that makes a **truly** invisible hem. Use a size 10 sharp needle and catch only a fiber of your fabric and make each stitch about ⅜" apart.

    Easier Way: Fuse hem with fusible web. (Test first for excess stiffness)

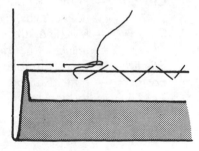

6. Slip stitch — used for jump hem in lining and to attach pockets. When the thread is pulled tight, everything disappears.

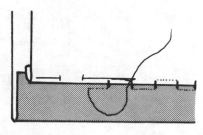

7. Stab stitch — a loose running stitch that joins two seams that fall on top of each other. Needle goes into well of seam on top at an angle and comes out of well on under layer. Used to attach upper collar/facing seam to under collar/jacket seam.

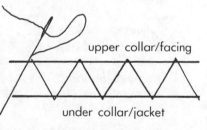

upper collar/facing

under collar/jacket

Easy, Easier, Easiest...Which One?

Be sure to read up on your fabric choice in "Sewing and Shaping Tips for Tailoring Fabrics" (see page 17) for additional help in deciding on a method. Remember though, we're biased! We try to use the "Easiest" Method whenever possible!

NOTE: You may use any method you wish for each jacket piece. If, however, you underline the front, you should also underline the back and sleeve for a consistent look.

Custom — Primarily hand made — uses good quality hair canvas.

Easy — Machine stitch hair canvas to an under-lining — hand pad stitch lapels.

Easier — Fuse a fusible interfacing to an underlining.

Easiest — Fuse a fusible interfacing directly to fashion fabric.

(Refer to page 9 for complete definitions)

Time Chart (in hours)

Task	Custom	Easy	Easier	Easiest
Cutting	3	3	3	1½
Fronts	10	6	4	1
Back	3	1	1	½
Collar	6	2	1	½
Sleeves	2	1	1	1
Bound Buttonholes	2	2	2	—
Lining	4	2	2	2
Finishing (Buttons, Buttonholes, Hems	3	1	1	1½
	33	18	15	8

The Pieces: Fronts
Custom Tailored

Be sure to use good quality hair canvas interfacing with a high wool content. Just ignore the underlining comments if you are not using one.

1.   Cut interfacing, (see page 27) underlining and fashion fabric. Snip mark center front, roll line, and collar placement on all three (see page 51). Cut dart out of interfacing.

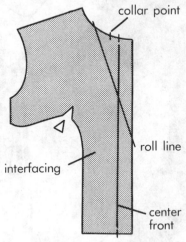

collar point

roll line

interfacing

center front

2.   **With** an underlining, mark darts and buttonholes on underlining only. **Without** an underlining mark darts and buttonholes on fashion fabric. Cut darts out of interfacing. Mark entire roll line, center front, and buttonholes on interfacing only.

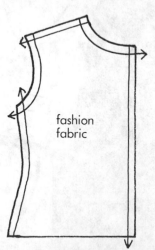

fashion fabric

3.   Directionally staystitch fashion fabric ½" from edge, all but bottom edge. The curved areas (bias) like the neck and armhole are a must!

NOTE: Staystitching seems like unnecessary extra work, but it's essential with loosely woven fabrics or a garment that will be handled a lot during construction. Staystitching is done to prevent stretching of cut edges. Stitch ½" from the edge in the direction shown.

4. Place underlining on fashion fabric, lining up snips. Press together to remove any wrinkles.

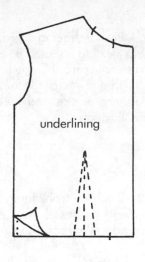

5. Glue layers together on all seam allowances except bottom and lapel (leave loose to allow for "turn-of-cloth," page 55).

6. Sew darts. If underlining, place pins through darts to prevent slippage. Machine baste through center of dart to hold layers together. Baste past point for a better hold and remove any stitches that show later. Then sew darts through all layers. Slash open and press flat (see page 39).

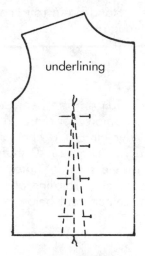

7. Make bound buttonholes now (see page 109).

8. Prepare dart in interfacing. Cut a bias strip of lightweight lining fabric 1" wide and 1" longer than dart, and sew edges to it. Sew bias strip to one side. Pivot, bring dart edges together and sew down other side.

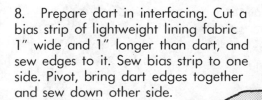

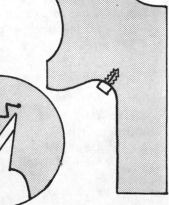

9. Pin interfacing to jacket front (bias strip next to jacket). Be sure roll line and center front snips line up.

Trim a rectangle out where buttonholes are and pull buttonhole lips through.

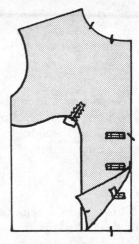

10. Trim ⅝" from interfacing in all but armhole seams if your pattern did not already eliminate them.

11. Hand baste roll line in place, through all layers.

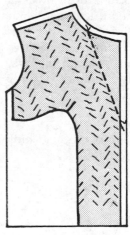

12. Tailor baste (see page 56) canvas to fashion fabric. Catch only underlining or a fiber of your fashion fabric. (Use size 10 sharp needle for invisible stitches.) Stitches should be parallel to roll line at top and parallel to center front below roll line.

13. Now tape roll line with ¼" twill tape. Place twill tape up against roll line, pull ¼" to ½" tighter (see page 54), and fell stitch in place (see page 57).

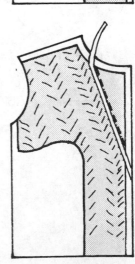

NOTE: You may leave a 3" extension of twill tape at the top. This will be attached to collar roll line for extra strength (see page 94).

14. Shape lapel by rolling it over a wash cloth that has been rolled into a sausage shape, and steam it. Allow it to cool and dry before moving.

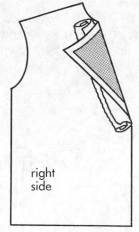

right side

15. Begin close to the roll line and pad lapel with stitches parallel to it, barely catching outside fabric (see page 56). Hold lapel over your hand to create a permanent roll. Make stitches ⅛" in length and ⅛" apart for a distance of ¾" from the roll line. Then they can be larger and ¼"-½" apart as you move to outside edge. Do not roll over hand as much as you approach outer edge or point will curl.

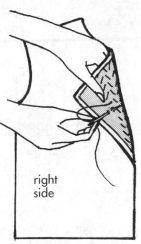

right side

16. Now tape neck and front edges with ½" seam tape (preshrunk). Place one edge against ⅝" seam line. Fell stitch (see page 57) both edges in place.

17. Remove roll line basting.

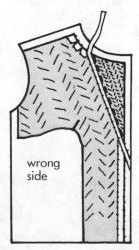

wrong side

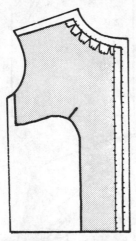

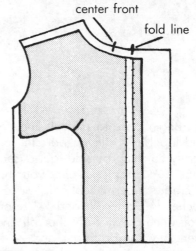

center front

fold line

Modified Speed-Taping Method:

A way to avoid hand taping and still eliminate bulky canvas from seam allowances in a garment with a separate facing. This method is excellent for velvet and velveteen.

1. Cut a strip of lightweight lining (Poly-SiBonne Plus is good.) 1" wide, same shape and grain as edge of front pattern piece.

2. After seam allowances have been trimmed from your interfacing, overlap lining ⅜" and glue-baste with glue stick.

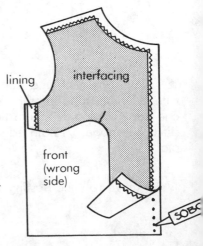

lining

interfacing

front (wrong side)

3. Stitch lining to edge of interfacing, lining side up, with one row of zig-zag or two rows of straight stitching.

4. Glue interfacing in place with Sobo.

5. Tailor baste interfacing, tape roll line. Continue as with Custom Front.

Front Piece: Easy

Machine baste interfacing to underlining

Must use an underlining. Be sure to use a hair canvas interfacing — any quality will work with this method.

1. Cut fashion fabric, under-lining, and interfacing. Snip mark center front, roll line, collar placement on all three.

2. Mark darts on underlining only. Cut darts out of interfacing. Mark entire roll line, center front, and button-holes on interfacing only.

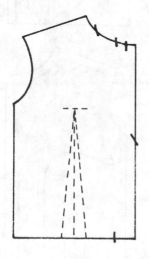

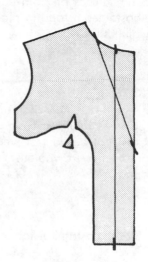

3. Place interfacing on underlining. Trim ⅝" from shoulder, neck, side and front of interfacing if pattern is not already trimmed. Glue-baste interfacing to underlining (dot over entire surface) with glue stick. This keeps interfacing from slipping while stitching. Let dry 5 minutes. (You may stitch through glue dots).

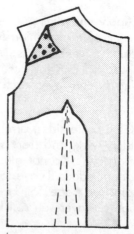

4. Machine stitch rows of stitching parallel to roll line and center front 1" apart, catching interfacing to underlining. If garment does not have a lapel, make all rows parallel to center front. Zig-zag or straight stitch around dart ¹/₁₆" from cut edge.

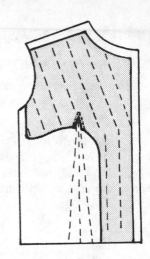

5. Stitch ½" seam tape to neck and front edges of interfacing and underlining, using straight or zig-zag machine stitches on both edges. May glue-baste seam tape in place first with glue stick.

NOTE: Taping is optional with this method since underlining will act as a stabilizer. However, coats that get lots of wear and loosely woven woolens should be taped.

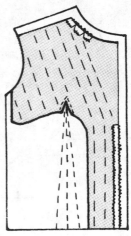

6. Staystitch fashion fabric.

7. Apply underlining/interfacing unit to wrong side of fashion fabric matching all snip marks. May double check both fronts for accuracy by placing pattern over each front.

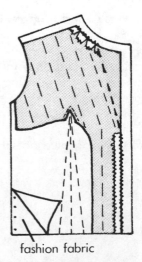

8. Glue-baste sides, armhole, shoulder, neck, and front with Sobo (see page 22). Do not glue-baste lapel or bottom edges. Leave loose for turn of cloth (see page 55). Hand baste through all layers on roll line.

fashion fabric

9. Sew darts through underlining and fashion fabric all in one (see page 61). Do not catch interfacing. Slash open and press. (See page 39).

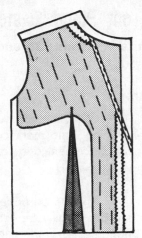

10. Tape roll line. Pull tighter by ¼"-½" (see page 54) and straight stitch or zig-zag in place.

NOTE: CHEAT! When machine taping the roll line, stitch the last two inches at the bottom by hand so your machine stitches won't show on the outside.

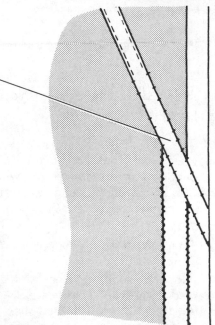

11. Roll lapel over wash cloth and steam into shape. (See page 63).

12. Hand pad lapels over your hand. (See page 63).

13. For bound buttonholes, trim away a rectangle ¼" wide and the length of the buttonholes in the area where buttonholes will be made to eliminate bulk. Make bound buttonholes now, machine buttonholes later (see page 108).

Front Piece: Easier

Fuse interfacing to underlining

You must use an underlining, but you may use any fusible interfacing depending on how much body is needed.

1.   Cut fashion fabric, underlining and interfacing. Snip mark center front, collar placement and roll line on all three.

2.   Mark darts on underlining only. Mark entire roll line, center front and buttonholes on interfacing only. Cut darts out of interfacing.

3.   Place interfacing on underlining. Line up snip marks.

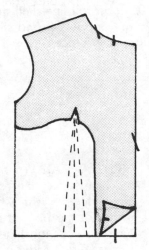

4.   Steam baste interfacing in place (slightly fuse — one second).

5.   Trim ⅝" off interfacing shoulder, side, neck and front. For bound buttonholes trim a rectangle ¼" wide and the length of the buttonhole out of buttonhole area.

6.   Fuse interfacing to underlining.

7.   Place ½" seam tape on front and neck edges next to seam line. Glue-baste tape in place with glue stick, clipping tape where necessary (see page 55). Straight stitch or zig-zag both edges of tape in place.

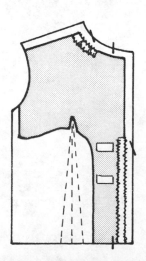

NOTE: Taping is optional here since underlining acts as a stabilizer. However, coats that get lots of wear should be taped.

8. Place underlining/interfacing unit on fashion fabric, lining up snips. Lay pattern on top of each front to check.

9. Glue-baste sides, armhole, shoulder, neck, and front with Sobo (see page 22). Do not glue-baste lapel or bottom edges. Leave loose for turn of cloth (see page 55).

10. Hand or machine baste through roll line bottom to top.

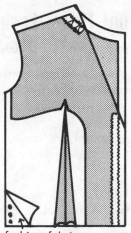

fashion fabric

NOTE: For a princess style front, trim and fuse interfacing to underlining before stitching as shown.

11. Directionally staystitch all but bottom and lapel.

12. Sew darts through underlining and fashion fabric (see page 61). Slash and press open.

13. Tape roll line. Pin ¼" twill tape next to roll line — pull tighter by ¼"-½" (see page 54) and zig-zag or straight stitch in place. Hand stitch last 2" so stitching line won't show on the outside. (See page 67).

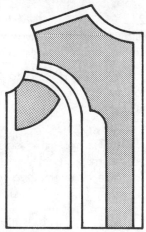

Princess style
front

14. Press lapel over rolled up wash cloth to shape it. No need to pad-stitch as fusible gives body — underlining and tape help it roll (see page 63).

15. Glue-baste (with Sobo) underlining to fashion fabric seam allowances in lapel area while lapel is still rolled over wash cloth. Allowing for "turn-of-cloth" helps create roll.

16. Make bound buttonholes now, machine buttonholes later.

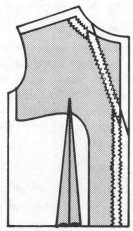

Front Piece: Easiest

Fuse interfacing to fashion fabric

Use any weight fusible interfacing and be sure to do a test sample. Check for amount of body fusible interfacing gives, and for a ridge on outside.

1. Cut fashion fabric. Mark darts. Cut interfacing (see page 27).

> **NOTE:** Pink inside edge of interfacing before fusing to make it less visible.

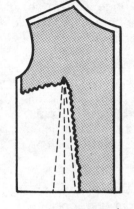

2. Trim away ½" of interfacing seam allowances, as shown, to reduce bulk. ⅛" is caught in seam line.

3. Fuse interfacing to fashion fabric following interfacing manufacturers instructions.

extra piece of interfacing

> **NOTE:** For extra body in lapel, you may steam baste an extra piece of interfacing to lapel under front interfacing. Make it ¼" smaller on outside edges and place against roll line.

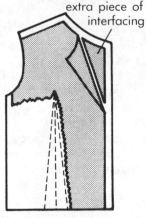

4. Machine stitch tape to roll line. (See page 67).

5. Because fusibles are thermoplastic, you can heat set them into any shape you wish. Shape lapel by rolling it over a wash cloth that has been rolled into a sausage shape, and steam press. Allow it to cool and dry before moving.

6. Sew darts.

7. Do bound buttonholes now, or machine buttonholes after jacket is finished.

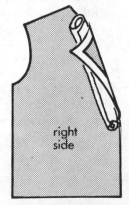

right side

Alternate Fusing Methods

(Trim ½" off seam allowances of interfacing.)

1. Fuse to front, facing, under collar, and upper collar: Fusing to all pieces as shown gives maximum shaping and body. It's great for lighter weight fabrics, ravelly fabrics, or just extra crispness.

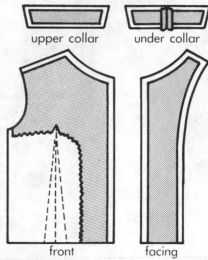

upper collar   under collar

front   facing

2. Fuse to entire front. Trim ½" off seam allowances of interfacing except in armhole, and cut dart out of interfacing.

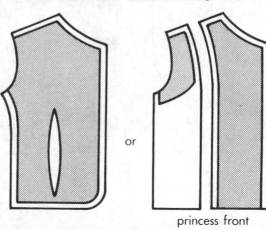

or

princess front

3. Fuse to facing and lapel only . . . a quick ready-to-wear method.

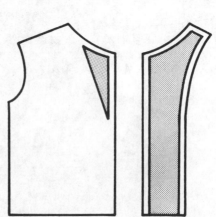

The Pieces: Backs

A "back stay" or back interfacing is absolutely necessary for a good looking, durable garment — remember your jacket spends 90% of its life on a hanger. The back stay is best cut straight grain in one piece from armhole to armhole in order to absorb "reaching stress". If a pattern piece is not included for a back stay, cut one according to instructions on page 27.

If your back stay is cut from a hair canvas, it is best to trim away seam allowances. However, if your fabric and back stay are not bulky, include them in the seam allowance — this eliminates hand catching seams to interfacing later.

Back Piece: Custom Method
(with or without an underlining)

1.   Cut fashion fabric, interfacing and underlining.

2.   Mark darts on underlining and interfacing (on fashion fabric if no underlining is used).

3.   Glue-baste underlining to fashion fabric. Staystitch each piece directionally where necessary.

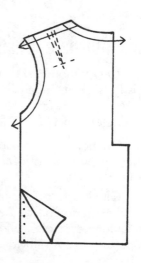

4.   Sew line of stitching through center of darts, stitch through both layers. Slash open and press.

5.   Sew center back seam and press open.

6.   Cut darts out of interfacing. Sew darts as on page 61.

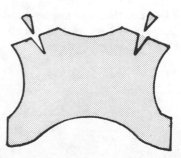

7. Place interfacing on back. Trim ⅝" off neck, shoulder, and underarm seams.

8. Using ½" seam tape, tape neck edge by hand. Use fell stitch (see page 57). Leave shoulders and sides of interfacing free as they will be caught in place later — simply pin to hold now.

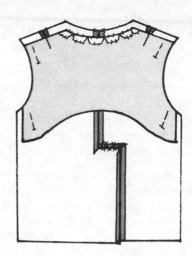

An Alternate Custom Method

This method may be used with lighter weight fabrics to save time — it is FASTER because neckline taping is eliminated. Use a lighter weight back stay fabric such as Veriform Durable Press or firm cotton broadcloth. Include it in all seams and darts.

1. Cut back stay according to instructions on page 27. Do not trim seam allowances off. Mark darts on back stay only.

2. Glue-baste back stay to fashion fabric unit on neck, shoulders, armholes, and underarm seam allowances.

3. Sew through center of darts. Sew darts through all thicknesses. Slash open and press.

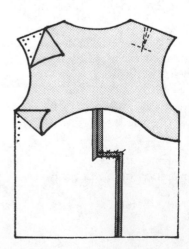

Back Piece: Easy/Easier Methods

These methods apply to an **underlined** jacket with a **one**-piece back **without a vent**. You may use the same interfacings as suggested in Custom or any medium to heavyweight fusible. Machine stitch (or fuse) the interfacing to the underlining, then underline the back unit.

1. Mark darts on underlining. Cut dart out of interfacing.

2. Place interfacing on underlining. Trim ⅝" seam allowances off neck, shoulder, and underarm if pattern did not eliminate them.

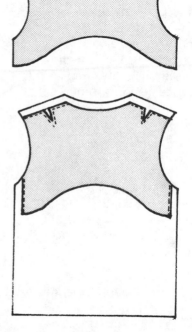

3. **EASY** — Glue-baste interfacing to armhole seam allowances with glue stick. Machine stitch ¹/₁₆" from edge of interfacing at dart, shoulder, and underarm to hold in place.

   EASIER — Use fusible inter-facing and fuse to underlining.

4. Machine stitch ½" seam tape to neck edge clipping as on page 55.

5. Glue-baste interfacing/underlining unit to fashion fabric with Sobo glue (see page 22).

Back Piece: Easiest Method

If you've selected a true 8 hour blazer fabric where your fusible interfacing cut edge does not leave a ridge on the right side, then fuse to the back too! Remember though, there are no darts or pockets on the back (like there are on the front) to camouflage the interfacing edge. We often fuse to the fronts, collar, etc, but use a stitchable interfacing across the back, using the Alternate Custom Method page 74.

If fusing, always do a test sample first to see if the fusible shows. Use a light or medium weight fusible and fuse to a one or two piece back as follows:

1. Cut back interfacing. Cut out darts. Trim ½" off neck, shoulders, and underarms. On a two piece back, also trim ½" off center back seam.

One piece back

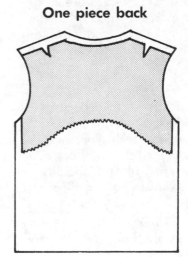

NOTE: To prevent ridge, pink bottom edge of interfacing before fusing.

2. Fuse interfacing to back.

3. Staystitch neck edge.

4. Stitch darts.

5. Sew center back seam.

Two piece back

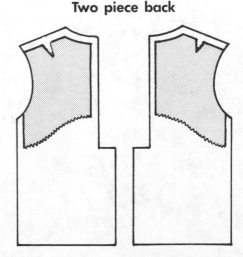

Back Vents

Interfacing a vent

Interface left vent for wrinkle resistance and to prevent stretching since it is the one that is on the outside. The right vent is left uninterfaced to reduce bulk. Also see hem interfacing techniques on page 97.

Custom method — interfacing is included in fold for a firm, crisp edge. Place interfacing ½" past vent fold and hem fold on garment side, and catch stitch interfacing in place. Use Veriform Durable Press or a hair canvas.

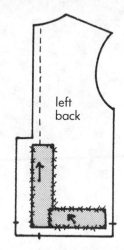

left
back

snip hemline

Easiest method — fuse interfacing to fold line of vent and hem. Trim ½" off outer edges.

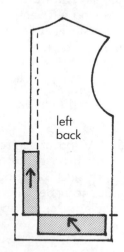

left
back

hem fold

NOTE: Hem interfacing is cut on the bias so that it will go **around** your body softly.

Sewing a vent

1. Sew center back seam to dot. Press open.

2. Snip right back seam allowance to center of last stitch.

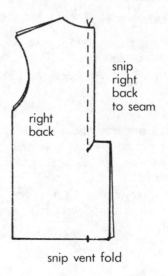

snip vent fold

3. Press toward left back, creasing left vent from center back stitching line to center back snips at bottom.

4. Press ⅝" seam allowance under on right vent.

5. At top of vent grade edges by trimming ¼" off right vent. Catch stitch both top edges in place to underlining or with fine needle to fashion fabric.

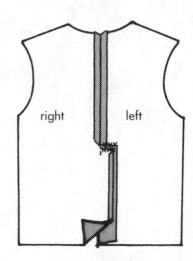

fold vent at snip

78

Mitering a vent

This is a super clean finish for the bottom of the left vent. Easy to do too! But caution — since this cannot be altered make **certain** your jacket is long enough or wait to miter vent until jacket is ready to finish.

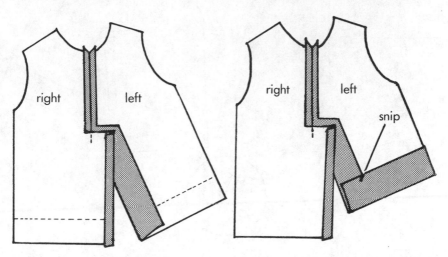

1. Fold left back vent from center back snip at bottom to center back seam line. Press.

2. Fold up hem allowance and snip intersection where edges meet.

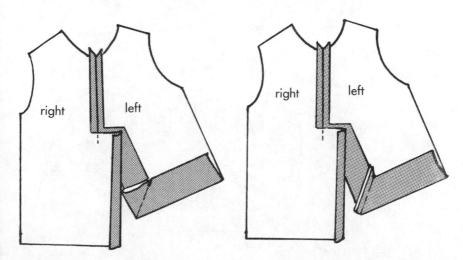

3. Unfold and line up snips.

4. Trim from snip to corner leaving ¼" seam allowances.

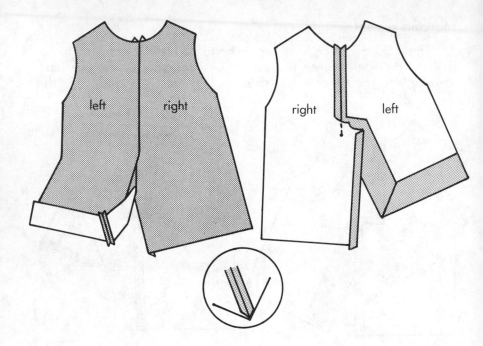

5.   Turn right sides together and stitch ¼" seam.

6.   Diagonally trim seam at corner to eliminate bulk. Turn and press.

7.   Turn lower edge of right back vent to outside along hem line. Stitch edges together on ⅝" seam line. Trim, turn and press.

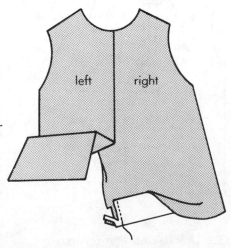

The Pieces: Collars
Custom Method

Upper Collar — Be sure to read about turn-of-cloth before cutting collars, page 55. Upper collar may be underlined to cushion outer seam allowances.

1. Press the two layers together.

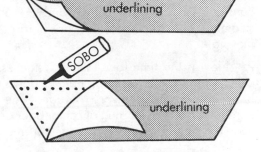

2. Glue baste — dot glue on seam allowances and pat together.

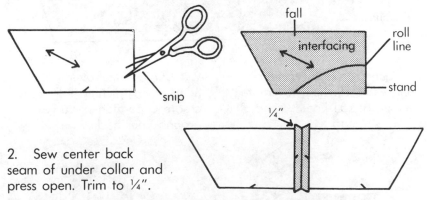

Under Collar — Follow cutting instructions on page 50.

1. Cut under collar and interfacing on bias. Mark roll line with snips on fashion fabric and with pencil or tracing wheel on interfacing.

2. Sew center back seam of under collar and press open. Trim to ¼".

3. Trim ⅝" off interfacing at center back and outside edges. Slip interfacing under center back seam allowance and catch stitch seam allowance to interfacing. Catch stitch outer edges of interfacing to collar.

4. Machine stitch center back seam allowances flat ⅛" from well of seam. This adds extra body to center back.

5. Hand baste on roll line barely catching outer fabric.

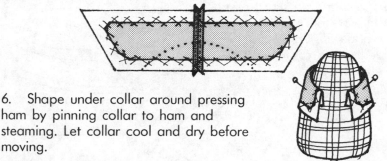

6. Shape under collar around pressing ham by pinning collar to ham and steaming. Let collar cool and dry before moving.

7. Now is the time for "TV-time" stitches. Hand pad stitch **stand** of collar with tiny stitches in an up and down direction, starting at center back and working toward outside edges. Pad stitch **fall** of collar parallel to roll line starting at center back on both sides. Use tiny stitches near roll line and larger ones as you move toward outer edges.

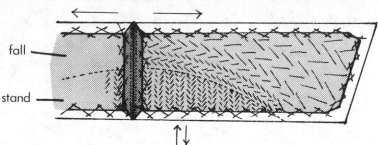

8. Curve collar over your hand while stitching to create a curve at roll line.

9. Curve collar over your hand while stitching fall to create a permanent curve around your neck.

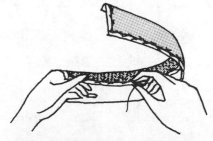

Easy Machine Method

Under collar —

1. Follow instructions 1 through 6 in Custom Method.

2. Machine padstitch vertically in stand and horizonatally in fall of collar using 12 stitches per inch. (You may use the "three-step" zig-zag on the fall of the collar.)

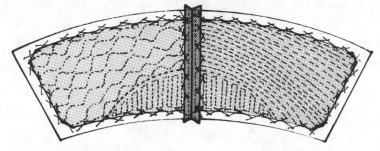

Easiest Fusible Method

Upper Collar (Optional) — Either glue or baste underlining as in custom collar, or fuse a lightweight fusible to upper collar. Trim ½" from outside edges.

Under Collar

1. Trim ½" off all edges of fusible interfacing. Fuse to each half of under collar. Snip roll line on fashion fabric and trace or pencil mark roll line on interfacing.

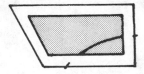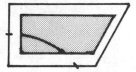

NOTE: If using a woven fusible, cut interfacing on bias. If using a nonwoven fusible, cut interfacing with stretch going around neck.

2. For extra body in the stand area, cut another piece of interfacing the same shape as collar stand. Trim ¼" smaller along roll line to allow for more accurate collar roll. Trim ½" off lower edge. Fuse to stand below roll line after center back seam is stitched, trimmed, and pressed open.

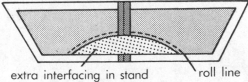

extra interfacing in stand   roll line

3. Pin to pressing ham and steam roll line as in Custom Method.

The Pieces: Sleeves

The "Easiest" sleeve is a one piece sleeve with an underarm seam, but a one or two piece sleeve with a vent is traditional in tailored jackets. However, we hear screams of frustration coming from the sewing room from those trying to get a professional vent finish. Our answer? Try the same **mitering technique** (stolen from menswear manufacturers!) used for the back vent, see page 79.

We recommend checking the sleeve length several times:

1.   Before cutting. Measure the sleeve and compare it to a jacket in your closet. Because of fashion variations in the sleeve cap (gathers, pleats, or tucks) which causes a change in the shoulder width, measuring the sleeve from top to hem is no longer accurate. Use the underarm measurement instead.

2.   During tissue fitting. (See page 44.) This is a very accurate way to judge sleeve length.

3.   Before mitering the vent. Stitch unvented front sleeve seam. Pin sleeve to jacket at underarm and shoulder only. Wrap sleeve around wrist and make sure hem fold line is at your wrist bone. If not, move hem fold marking until length is correct.

Cutting and Marking

1.   Most vented sleeve patterns look like this one. To miter vent, upper sleeve vent extension edge should be filled in to end at sleeve hem edge, as illustrated.

2.   Cut sleeves. Snip notches, underarm dots, and shoulder dot at top of upper sleeve. Also snip hem folds.

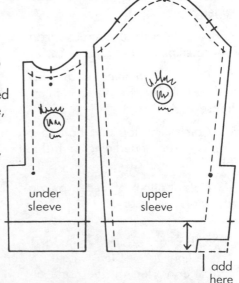

under sleeve

upper sleeve

add here

NOTE: Did you know that one notch always means FRONT of sleeve and two notches always mean BACK of sleeve?

Sew Sleeve

Glue underlining (if using one) in place on all but hem edges before sewing sleeve.

1. Sew side front seam. Press open.

2. Machine baste 2 rows across top of sleeve, notch to notch, one row on ⅜ and one on ⅝", or one row on ½" and one row on ¾" (¾" row will be removed later, see page 89).

3. Trim seam in hem area to ¼".

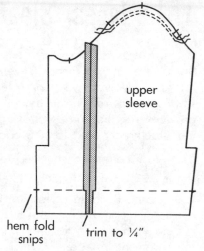

upper sleeve

hem fold snips   trim to ¼"

Prepare Hem

1. Cut a bias strip of interfacing (light to medium weight stitchable, see page 24) 1" wider than hem width.

2. Place interfacing ½" below fold line of sleeve. Trim ⅝" off outer edges.

3. Press hem up and crease from snip to snip.

4. Do a long running stitch along fold to hold interfacing to hem crease.

5. Catch-stitch top and bottom of interfacing to underlining or fashion fabric.

6. Finish bottom of sleeve by zig-zagging if necessary.

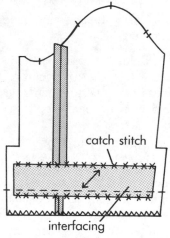

catch stitch

interfacing

NOTE: For "Easiest" method, fuse light to medium weight fusible interfacing (see page 6) to foldline on hem allowance. Trim away ½" where shown.

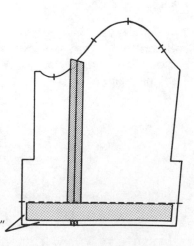

trim ½"

Mitered Vent

The upper vent on the upper sleeve (double-notched side) may be mitered for a clean finish. Under vent is not mitered.

1. Fold on vent fold line, then fold hem up. Snip corner where they come together.

2. Pull fold out and line up snips. Trim to ¼" from snips to corner (see page 79).

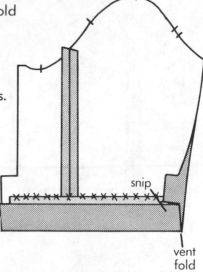

snip

vent fold

3. Turn right sides together and stitch ¼" seam from snips to corner. Slash across corner to eliminate bulk and press seam open (see page 80).

4. Fold hem up on underlap side at hem snip, right sides together, and stitch ¼" seam. Trim seam, slash across corner.

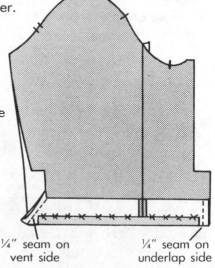

¼" seam on vent side

¼" seam on underlap side

5. Turn to inside and press.

Finish Sleeve

1. You can hem sleeves flat before sewing second seam! You may pin hem and seam and try on for a fitting at this point.

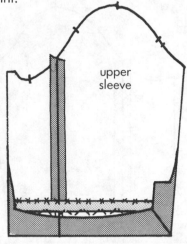

upper sleeve

2. Sew sleeve seam to dot. Clip underlap side to dot.

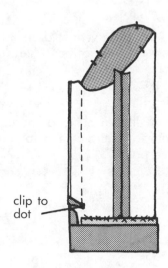

clip to dot

3. Press seam open over seam roll and catch stitch top and sides of vents in place.

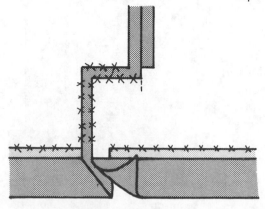

4. Sew 2 to 4 buttons on through both layers. (Small, closely spaced buttons are super!)

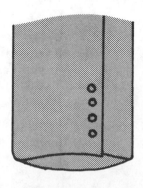

NOTE: Some patterns say to put bound or machine buttonholes in vent — ugh! Unnecessary!

Setting in a Sleeve — Method I

1. Machine baste two rows of stitching from notch to notch over the sleeve cap.

Pati's Way
Place one row at ⅜" from the edge and the other at ⅝". Pull on ⅜" stitching only, forming cap. ⅝" line acts only as a final stitching guide.

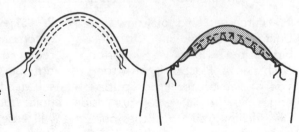

Susan's Way
Place one row at ½" from the edge and the other at ¾". Pull up both rows equally, final stitch between easing threads at ⅝". Remove ¾" basting.

   Set in sleeve by pinning in place and machine basting. Try on for fit, adjust if needed (see page 91), permanent stitch again on ⅝" and ¼".

2. Trim seam under arm to ¼" from notch to notch.

3. Always press sleeve cap from the inside. Do not top-press the cap.

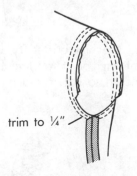

trim to ¼"

4. Bias strips (1½" wide, 12" long) of lambswool, Canvas Unlimited, or Pellon Fleece stitched to the seam line of the sleeve cap from notch to notch over the sleeve cap will fill out the cap and give it the desired shape.

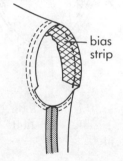

bias strip

Setting in a Sleeve — Method II

The sound of the term "setting in a sleeve" often makes the strongest soul quake — and it shouldn't. Read on to find out about a great new way to get a PUCKER FREE set-in sleeve! We first discovered it as a sure-fire way to set in a sleeve in Ultrasuede®.

1. Purchase ⅜ yd. of Canvas Unlimited or Armo-Rite. Cut one bias strip 12" long, 1½" wide for each sleeve. Place strip on wrong side of sleeve cap, lining up top edges. Sew to sleeve cap just inside ⅝" stitching, using 6 stitches per inch, stretching bias to its fullest while stitching.

2. Sleeve cap is automatically eased and ready to sew into armhole. Even if sleeve is still a bit large for arm-hole, additional fullness will ease in smoothly. Press from inside cap to shrink in ease.

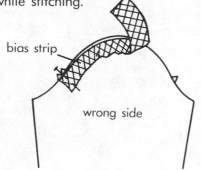

bias strip

wrong side

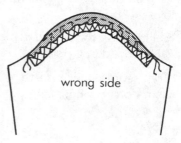

wrong side

3. Pin and stitch sleeve into jacket armhole. Machine baste. Try on for fit, adjust if needed (see page 91). Permanent stitch on ⅝" and reinforce stitch on ¼". Trim seam allowance from notch to notch under arm.

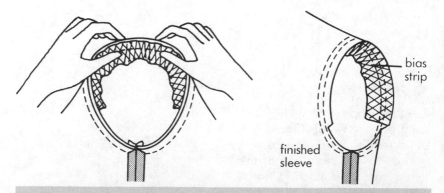

bias strip

finished sleeve

NOTE: This technique also works on blouse and dress weight fabrics, simply substitute Seams Great or Seams Saver for Canvas Unlimited.

Fine Tune Sleeve Fit

1. Baste sleeve into jacket armhole using "Setting in a Sleeve Method I or II."

2. Try on jacket over same weight clothing you will wear under jacket. Lap center fronts. Pin. Slip shoulder pads under jacket. Pin in place.

3. **Fullness in the wrong place?** If there are puckers or pulls, clip basting from the outside and pull seam apart. Readjust fullness until you eliminate puckers. Some bodies require more front or back sleeve fullness. The pattern gives you an average placement of fullness, so you must tailor this to your body's special needs.

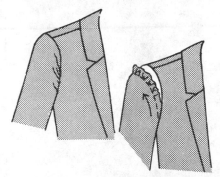 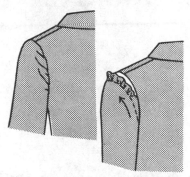

move fullness toward back   move fullness toward front

4. **Too much fullness?** Tightly woven fabrics, those with a permanent press finish, and some synthetics are more difficult to ease. Since your sleeve pattern has been designed for an "average" fabric, you may find you have too much sleeve for too little armhole.

First, try sewing the sleeve into the armhole again — a fuller cap will produce a better fit — but if you still have puckers, cheat!!

Remove basting from notch to notch over sleeve cap. Slip sleeve ¼" further into armhole. Pin. Baste at garment ⅝". Now it should look better, but remember, you are sacrificing some ease for a better looking sleeve. Sometimes a necessity!

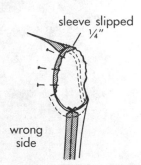

sleeve slipped ¼"

wrong side

Putting All The Pieces Together

It is best to follow general pattern instructions when sewing a jacket or coat together, however this is the construction order we think is the most efficient. We have also included some super tips most patterns just don't have room to show you.

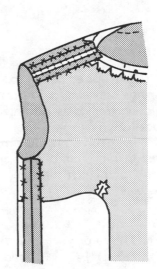

1. **Sew front to back** at shoulder and sides. Catch stitch shoulder and side seams to interfacing. (Optional in "Easiest" method.)

2. **Tape shoulders** (unless interfacing is included in seam for stability as in "Easier" and "Easiest" methods). Center ½" seam tape over shoulder seam and fell stitch in place.

3. **Attach under collar to garment**

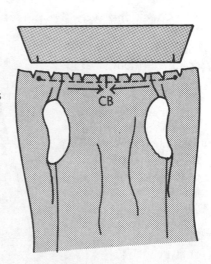

- Clip to staystitching.
- Sew under collar to garment from dot to dot, stitching from dots to center back (CB).
- Press seam open over long curve on the June Tailor board. (See page 36).
- Trim seam allowances to ¼". Catch stitch in place if needed to keep flat.

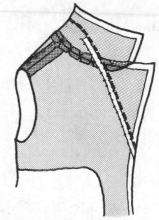

NOTE: If a 3" extension was left on the roll line twill tape (page 62), fell stitch it to collar (below roll line).

4. **Sew upper collar to facings** between large dots, stitching from dots to center back (CB). Press seam open over long curve on June Tailor board. Trim seam allowances to ⅜" and catch stitch in place.

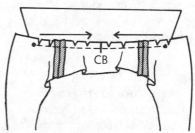

NOTE: Attach lining unit to upper collar/facing unit now if using the Quick Lining method. (See page 103).

5. **Set sleeves into garment.** (See pages 89, 90).

6. **Attach shoulder pads.** (See page 99).

7. **Check the way the pieces fit together.** Place upper collar/facing unit on under collar/garment, wrong sides together. Hang on a hanger to see if the lapels and collars fall correctly. Pin through gorge lines to hold them in place. Make sure facing is the same length as jacket bottom. If not, trim until even.

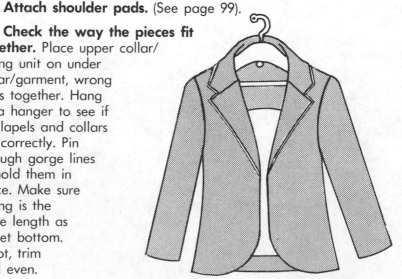

8. **Pin upper collar/facing unit to under collar/ garment unit** right sides together.

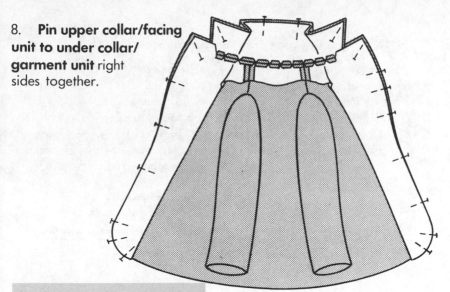

NOTE: Make a "Tailor's Blister" in order to get rid of excess fabric in upper collar and upper lapel points which have been cut larger to allow for "turn of the cloth". Pin a small tuck about ½" from point. Remove pin after outer seams have been stitched.

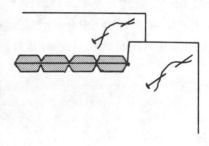

9. **Stitch outer edges together.** Use 20 stitches per inch at all corners and curves where close trimming is required.

Move seam allowances out of way. Stitch from dot to center back of collar on each side, taking 2 stitches diagonally across corner.

Move all seam allowances toward collar. Stitch from dot to bottom of jacket, taking 2 stitches diagonally across corner.

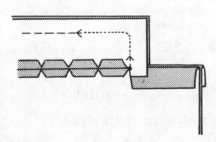

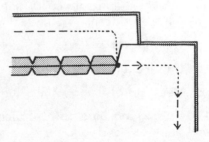

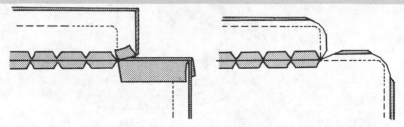

10. **Clip to seam line at bottom of roll line** so lapel will roll better.

11. **Press all seams open** over proper pressing equipment.

12. **Turn with point turner and top press.** Roll seams to under side, press, flatten with pounding block.

13. **Stabstitch collar seams together** through wells of upper and under collar seams. (See page 57).

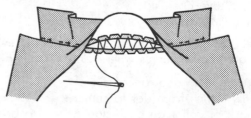

CHEAT — If the upper collar is not large enough to go over under collar so that outer seams won't show (not enough "turn-of-cloth" allowance) — slip upper collar until it is large enough. Anchor at that point instead of centering under/upper collar seams.

14. **Hem jacket** (see page 97) unless "Quick Lining" (see page 103).

15. **Line jacket.** (See page 101).

16. **Hem jacket lining** with a jump hem. (See page 105).

17. **If using machine buttonholes, make them now.** Apply buttons and finish all handwork.

Hems

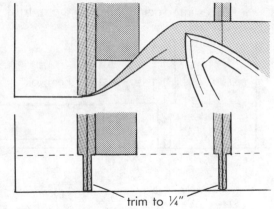

1. Turn up hem and lightly press in a crease at hem fold line.

2. Trim all seam allowances in hem area to ¼".

trim to ¼"

3. Interface hem using the custom or easiest method. (You may have already interfaced the back hem and back vent. See page 77).

Interface Hem — Custom Method

• Cut a strip of bias interfacing (light to medium weight woven) 1" wider than hem allowance and long enough to go around hem and lap ¼" over front interfacings.

• Place interfacing ½" beyond hem fold and lap ¼" over front interfacing. Snip interfacing at seams and slip under seam allowances. Baste to fashion fabric at fold line, but do not stitch through to outside.

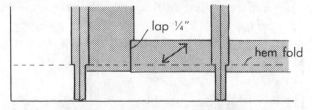

lap ¼"

hem fold

• Catch stitch hem interfacing to front interfacing and to garment at top and bottom edges.

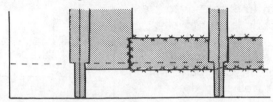

Interface Hem — Easiest Method

• Cut a bias strip (cut crosswise with nonwovens) of light to medium weight fusible interfacing the width of the hem minus ½", and long enough to go around hem and ¼" past front interfacing.

• Place interfacing next to hem fold line and fuse to hem allowance.

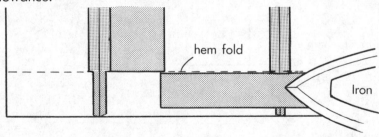

hem fold

Iron

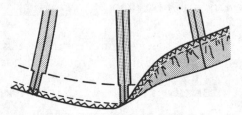

4. If hem is curved, machine baste ¼" from edge and ease hem to fit garment.

5. Finish hem edge if fabric is very ravelly or garment is unlined. Zig-zag or use a seam finish for unlined jackets as on page 31.

6. Turn up hem and press. **Do not press over top edge**. You will get a crease that will show on the outside.

7. Remove bulk from facing area by trimming as shown. Catch stitch hem to facings and interfacing as shown and blind hem rest of jacket.

CUSTOM   **EASIEST**

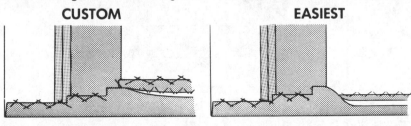

7. Catch stitch front facings to hem. If your fabric is very ravelly, run a thin line of Fray Check along the facing cut edge, then catch stitch over edge. If your fabric will not ravel, don't bother to do anything.

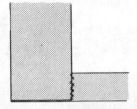

NOTE: A curved blazer-type front is handled in the same manner, but it's easier than the square front because the lower edge of the front facing is automatically finished after stitching around, trimming, grading, notching and turning lower curve.

Shoulder Pads

Shoulder pads are important for smooth shaping in a tailored garment, and you don't have to look like a football player in them! If you are square shouldered, just use a thinner pad than the pattern suggests. If you can't find the right size you can make your own. If you have sloping shoulders and don't want that droopy look, buy a shoulder pad that is thicker than suggested. To level out uneven shoulders, don't alter the pattern, just use thicker and thinner pads!

The pattern designer raises the shoulder to fit the size pad she recommends. However, when the designer calls for a ¾" pad, she has raised the shoulder only ⅜"-½" since most pads will compact. During the first fitting of your jacket, try on with shoulder pad slipped in place. If pulls or drag lines appear, you can change shoulder pad thickness, or raise or lower the shoulder seam (see page 46).

What the shoulder pad package never tells you!

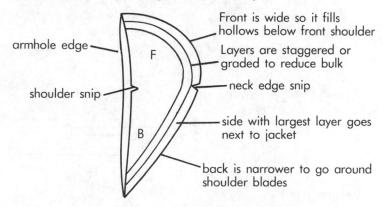

armhole edge

F

shoulder snip

B

Front is wide so it fills hollows below front shoulder

Layers are staggered or graded to reduce bulk

neck edge snip

side with largest layer goes next to jacket

back is narrower to go around shoulder blades

How to sew in a shoulder pad

1. Turn jacket inside out and place pad on jacket, aligning shoulder seams. Pad should extend ¼"-⅜" into conventional sleeve cap, and up to 1" into pleated or darted sleeve caps. (The designer has made the shoulder narrower and considers the wider cap part of the shoulder). Pin in place.

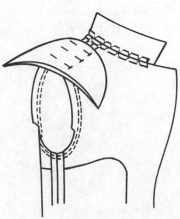

2. Turn jacket to **right side**, smooth shoulder pads in place and anchor with pins. This is the only way to insure the pad will fit the inside curve and be smooth when you wear the jacket. Try on.

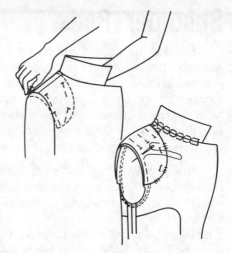

3. Turn to wrong side and loosely stitch pad to interfacing (make sure these stitches are invisible on jacket right side) and to armhole seam allowance. Remove pins.

Make shoulder pads the "No-Sew" way!

Make your own shoulder pads if:
- you want one that is thinner or thicker than you can buy
- you want one that covers a larger area
- you need a custom-shaped pad to fill in a hollow chest

1. Cut one or more triangles of polyester fleece, layer as shown for your desired thickness.

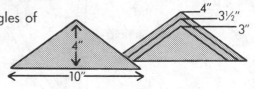

2. Place on fusible side of a 9" × 11" layer of Easy-Knit. Fuse all edges together.

3. Trim excess Easy-Knit away to within ¼" of the fleece. Easy-Knit will not ravel, so finishing is unnecessary.

NOTE: For a custom-shaped pad, lap shoulder seamline of jacket front and back pattern pieces and draw the shape you need. Cut out of fleece. Place additional layers of fleece in any area that needs to be built up. Cover with Easy-Knit, fuse, trim to within ¼" of fleece.

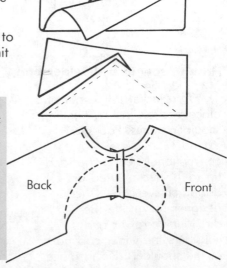

Back   Front

Lining...Three Methods

1. **Custom** — done almost entirely by hand, is good with heavy fabrics that are awkward to handle at the machine. The lining fits inside the jacket best with this method.

2. **Quick Lining** — a super-fast machine method that gives great results!

3. **Combination method** — gives a fast machine-stitched lining but yet a custom fit in the shoulder area. Just follow Quick Lining steps but attach the lining sleeve to the garment by hand.

Custom Method

1. Cut lining as shown on page 30.

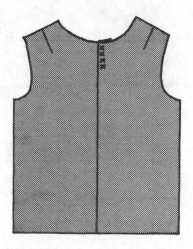

2. Stitch darts and back seam, press pleat to one side and tack with cross stitches below neckline.

3. Stitch all side seams, press open. Staystitch at ½", press under front, shoulder and neck seam allowances, clip and notch where necessary.

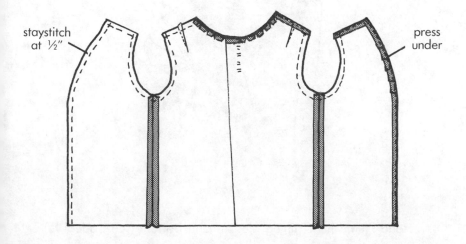

staystitch at ½"

press under

4. Pin lining into body of garment by lining up underarm seams and shoulder seams.

5. Slipstitch fronts, neckline, shoulders. Baste armhole edges together, trim lining to match garment armhole.

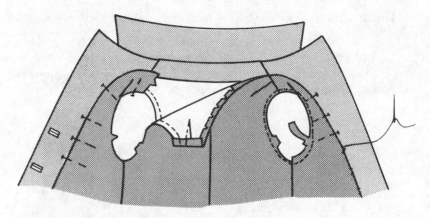

6. Stitch sleeve seam, press open. Easestitch sleeve cap, staystitch underarm area.

7. Slip sleeve lining over armhole, match notches and sleeve top dot. Pull ease stitching threads until lining fits sleeve comfortably. Clip or trim underarm area as needed. Slip stitch lining sleeve cap in place.

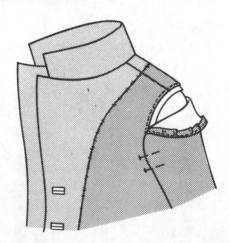

8. Hand "jump hem" lining sleeves and bottom (see page 105).

"Quick Lining" Method

1. Assemble all garment pieces — back, front, and sleeves. (Sleeves should already be hemmed.) Stitch under collar to body of garment. Do not hem jacket yet.

2. Assemble all lining pieces — back, front, and sleeves. Remember sleeve and body underarm seam allowances should be cut ¼" higher. If not cut this way, stitch ⅜" underarm seam to compensate. (See page 30).

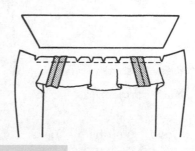

3. Assemble facing unit, attach upper collar to staystitched and clipped neckline.

NOTE: To add a custom touch to your lining, baste **PRESHRUNK** piping or decorative edging to facing ⅝" stitching line. A zipper foot helps you stitch closest to trim. Continue with step 4. Voila! a beautiful trim peeking out next to the lining!

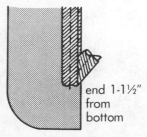

end 1-1½" from bottom

4. Sew facing/upper collar unit to lining using ⅝" seam, and stopping 3-4" from bottom of facing.

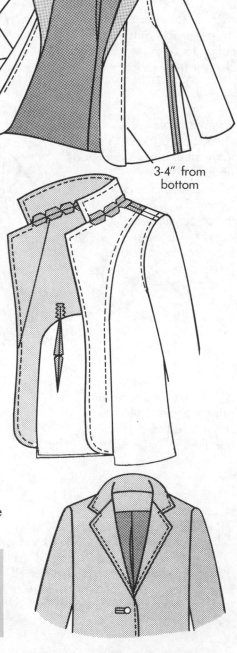

3-4" from bottom

5. Place collars right sides together. Pin remaining front edges together. Stitch outside edges together. Trim, layer, clip, notch, and slash seams where necessary. Turn garment right side out.

6. Press finished garment.

7. Hem garment (see page 97).

8. Hand "jump hem" lining sleeves and bottom (see page 105).

NOTE: Hand tack lining at front of armhole to prevent facing from creeping at front edge.

Hemming the Lining

"Jump" hem at jacket bottom (gives lining moving room)

1. Make sure lining is cut to the length of the hemmed, finished garment.

2. Turn lining hem under until raw edge matches top edge of garment hem.

3. Pin in place about 1" from bottom fold of lining.

4. Lift hem fold and slipstitch, catching only the hem allowance of the lining and not the lining itself. Smooth extra length downward to form "jump" or pleat. Finish slipstitching front edges of lining to facing.

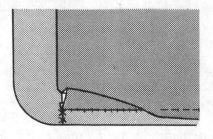 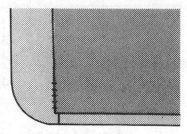

"Jump" hem in a sleeve

1. Turn back bottom edge of sleeve. (It's easier to handle like this since sleeve is a small cylinder.)

2. Turn lining hem edge under ⅝" and match raw edges to top of sleeve hem.

3. Slipstitch in place. A "jump" hem or pleat will automatically be created.

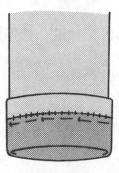

The Goof-Proof Back Vent in a Lining

Have you ever had problems figuring out which side of the lining in the vent area to cut away? This one is Goof-Proof!

NOTE: Left and right refer to when the jacket is on your back. A vent is like a lapped zipper — it laps left over right.

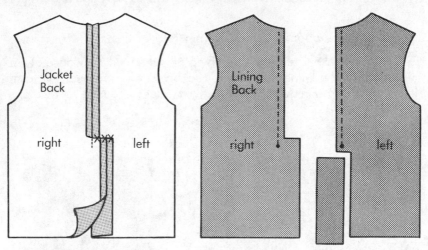

1. Cut lining

2. Mark cut-away section (as on pattern) with tracing paper on both back pieces. Do not cut anything out of vent area yet.

3. Sew center back seam to large dot.

4. Lay lining on jacket wrong sides together. Cut away left back.

Finishing Back Vent

For an easy-to-do, flat look, even designers have decided machine topstitching the edges of the under vent is best.

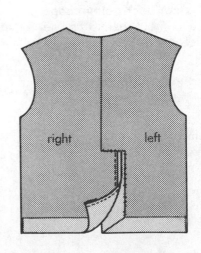

1. Assemble lining as on page 101 or 103.

2. Save work — machine stitch right vent and lining edges together (Calvin Klein does!). (Hand slip stitch top of vent and left side.)

Super Touches For a Custom Look!

Machine Buttonholes

Standard sewing machine buttonholes are great in casual jackets, in children's things, and where bound buttonholes may not be worth the time spent. Bound buttonholes are traditional in dressy suits and coats, keyhole buttonholes are generally used in blazers and menswear, and we tend to use machine buttonholes wherever we can!

Prevent stretch in buttonholes:

• Stabilize — "Tear-away" interfacing or a patch of no stretch interfacing stitched under the buttonhole will help control stretch.

• Cord — Stitch buttonholes over cording or a heavy-weight thread. Leave a loop at the end. When buttonhole is completed pull on cording ends until loop disappears. With a hand sewing needle, bring loose cord ends to wrong side. Tie and clip.

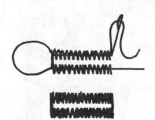

Keyhole Buttonholes

If you have a keyhole attachment on your machine, use it for a sporty blazer look as designers are doing now. OR, find a tailor — they charge $4 to $5 per hand keyhole buttonhole. A beautiful touch and worth every penny!

Bound Buttonholes

Bound buttonholes are beautiful and durable and not hard to make once you develop a "system." We had to laugh when our artist Priscilla described a bound buttonhole — "It's just 3 lines." Well, it's not **quite** as easy as an artist's concept but here are two favorite methods.

NOTE: All horizontal buttonholes begin ⅛" toward edge from center front.

Mark Carefully!

Using tracing paper or a water soluble marker and a ruler, mark the center and ends of buttonhole on the interfacing side. Machine baste on these lines through interfacing and fashion fabric to transfer markings to right side. Use a contrasting color thread for easy-to-see markings.

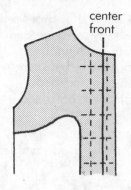

center front

Bound Buttonhole — Susan's Favorite Method

NOTE: Always make a sample first to test the fashion fabric performance and buttonhole size (slip button through to make sure it fits!)

1. Mark fabric as shown above.

2. Cut a strip of fabric the length of the buttonhole plus 1", and about 1½" wide. Strip may be straight grain or bias.

NOTE: A faster way — Cut one long strip for all buttonholes. Snip apart as needed.

3. Corded buttonholes look best in everything but the very heaviest coatings, because they don't stretch or sink into the hole. To cord, fold strip in half, wrong sides together. Place small string or cording (preshrunk) in the fold.

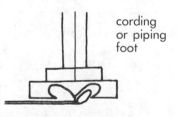

cording or piping foot

Assemble cording/piping foot or zipper foot so the needle hits just next to the cord. Tuck corded edge into cording foot tunnel, machine stitch — should produce a ⅛" corded piping.

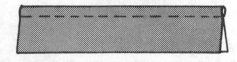

4. To aid stitching and reduce bulk, trim one raw edge to the exact width of the stitched cord.

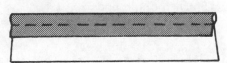

5.   Center strip over vertical basting lines on the garment right side, with short raw edge against **horizontal** basting line. Stitch, on top of original stitching, using a short stitch, between the vertical markings. Backstitch at each end.

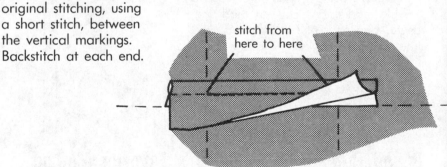

stitch from
here to here

6.   Place raw edge of second strip against the first strip raw edge. The two untrimmed edges now form a "tent". Look for the tent! Stitch on top of original stitching between vertical markings.

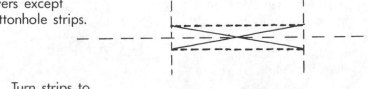

stitch from
here to here

7.   From wrong side, clip an X through all layers except buttonhole strips.

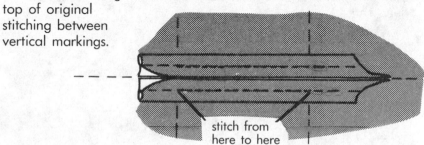

8.   Turn strips to inside — tug lightly on strips to straighten lips and corners. Fold back fashion fabric exposing ends.

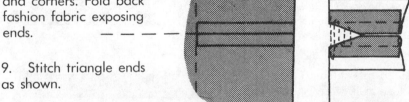

9.   Stitch triangle ends as shown.

10. Finish facing as shown on page 114.

Bound Buttonhole — Pati's Favorite Method

1. **Pin bias strips** of matching lining (such as Poly-SiBonne Plus, or use coordinated crisp fabrics like silk organza or cotton organdy) 1" longer than buttonhole and 1½" wide on right side of garment, centered over placement lines.

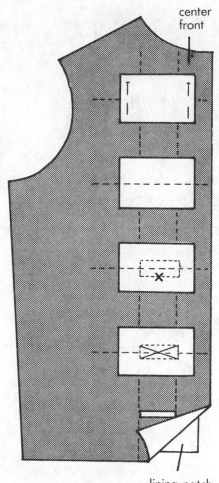

center front

lining patch

2. **Machine baste** through center of lining. (Easiest when done from wrong side — just follow basting lines.)

3. **Using small stitches,** stitch a rectangle the length of the buttonhole and ¼" wide (⅛" on either side of the center line). Use the edge of metal presser foot as a stitching guide. Start and stop stitching at "X" to avoid weak corners. Check each rectangle — they must be on grain, the same size, and have square corners. Remove basting.

4. **From wrong side** trim interfacing out of rectangle to eliminate bulk.

5. **Clip rectangle** to corners.

> **NOTE:** Clip from **center to corner** to form larger wedges at each end.

111

6. **Turn lining to wrong side** to form "window". Press.

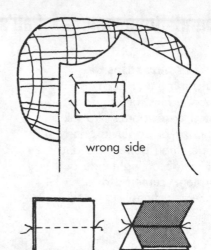

wrong side

7. **Prepare lips** by basting through the center of two pieces of fashion fabric, right sides together. Lips should be on straight of grain unless fashion fabric is plaid — then use bias.

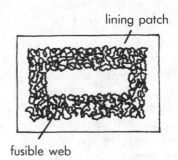

8. **Center lips under window** and baste in place. A speedy method for centering lips is to steam baste them in place with fusible web. Cut a piece of fusible web with a rectangle cut out of the center the size of buttonhole window.

lining patch

fusible web

NOTE: To cut a window in the web, fold the rectangle in half and clip out a piece half the length of the buttonhole and ¼" wide.

Place the web on the wrong side of buttonhole over the lining patch. "Steam baste" web in place by lightly steaming web until it becomes tacky and adheres to lining patch. (**Do not touch** iron to web!)

9. **From right side,** center lips under window and fuse using a press cloth. Lips will now stay in place without slipping while stitching.

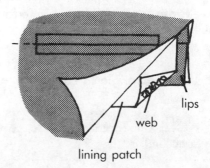

lips

web

lining patch

10. **Fold back fashion fabric,** exposing long sides of lining patch. Using a zipper foot, stitch lining to lips. Do both long sides, then triangular ends. Stitch across triangle several times to anchor, as shown.

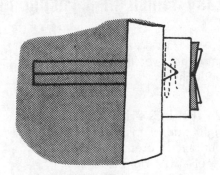

NOTE: For SPEED, do the same end of all the buttonholes at one time continuously.

11. **Trim and grade** back side of buttonhole. Hand catch stitch to interfacing. This is especially important for bulky fabrics.

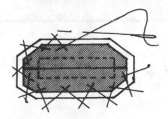

Buttons

Sewing on buttons with a shank is especially important in tailoring due to the bulk of the fabric.

• Sew button on over a toothpick.

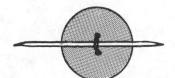

• Remove toothpick and wrap thread 5-10 times around shank. Knot.

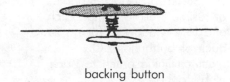

• Use a clear plastic backing button for added strength.

backing button

Easy Finish in a Facing for a Bound Buttonhole

1. Pin facing in place smoothly over the back of buttonholes.

2. Put bias strips of lining on right side of facing over buttonhole area. (Do this by "feel" from right side of garment and use 2" × 3" pieces of lining to make sure they cover buttonhole area.)

3. Stick pins straight down through ends of buttonholes.

4. Draw a pencil line on lining patch from pin to pin. This marks the center of the buttonhole.

5. Place two additional pins across ends of buttonholes and take first pins out.

6. Machine baste over center line from pin to pin.

7. Stitch a rectangle and clip to corners.

8. Turn lining patch to wrong side and press.

9. Steam baste a rectangle of fusible web to lining patch and fuse window in facing to back of buttonhole. Or, slipstitch lining patch to back of buttonhole.

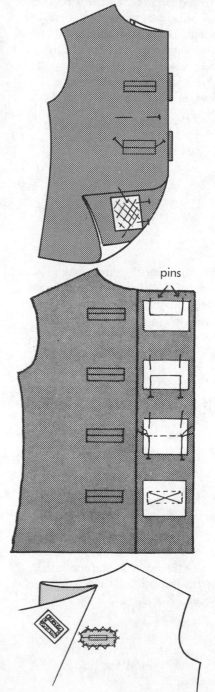

pins

Super-Duper Double Welt Pocket

1. This is a double welt (often placed on a slant on a jacket for a more slimming effect). Notice welt ends are straight grain. Slip a lined pocket flap into a welt and it becomes a traditional **flapped** menswear type double welt pocket. Pocket flap ends are also straight grain.

2. If you could see through the jacket you would see the pocket lining at the same angle as your hand going in.

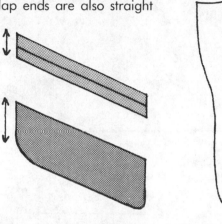

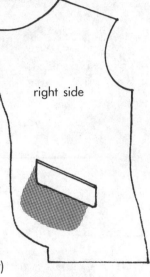

right side

Instructions (for each standard 6" pocket)

1. **Welt** — cut a rectangle of fashion fabric 3" wide and 8" long. (For pocket **without flap,** cut 2 of these for each pocket.)

2. **Lining** — cut a piece of lining for pocket 8" wide and 15-18" long. Sew wrong side of welt piece to right side of lining, matching top raw edges. Stitch. Zig-zag over lower raw edge as shown. (For pocket **without flap,** stitch second fashion fabric rectangle to opposite end.)

3. **Pellon stabilizer** — cut a piece of Featherweight Pellon (**not fusible**) the same size as the welt.

4. Pencil 2 parallel lines the length of the Pellon, centered, ½" apart.

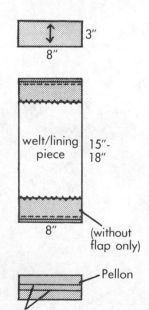

3"

8"

welt/lining piece 15"-18"

8"

(without flap only)

Pellon

pencil lines

115

5. **On wrong side of jacket,** mark pocket placement lines. End lines should be on straight of grain. (All illustrations will show pocket **with flap**)

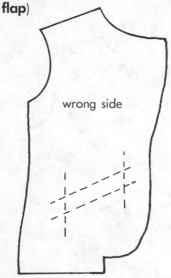

wrong side

6. **On wrong side of jacket,** place Pellon piece. Draw end lines on Pellon at placement markings on jacket, forming a "box". Stitch with small stitches around box. Start and stop stitching in center of pocket at X, not at a corner.

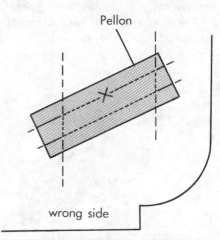

Pellon

wrong side

NOTE: All future permanent stitching will be on the Pellon box stitching lines, done from the wrong side.

7. **On right side of jacket,** center welt/lining piece over straight lines. Pin in place.

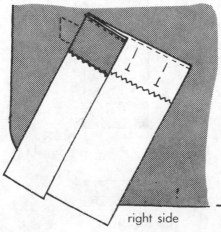

right side

8. **From wrong side,** stitch on top of stitching lines on **long** sides of box only, stop at ends. Carefully backstitch on top of last stitch.

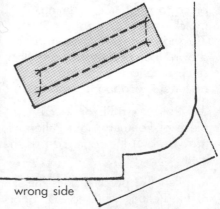

wrong side

9. **From wrong side,** make 2 rows of basting stitches ¼" above and below the box through all layers.

NOTE: Basting lines are always half the width of stitched box.

10. **From right side,** fold pocket up firmly against basting line, press, pin in place.

From wrong side, stitch again on lower long side of Pellon box — just follow previous stitching line and end exactly at ends of box. Backstitch carefully. This will create the "welt".

From right side this is what you will see after stitching.

11. **On right side,** fold upper part of welt down, press and pin. **From wrong side,** stitch on upper line of box. Backstitch at end carefully.

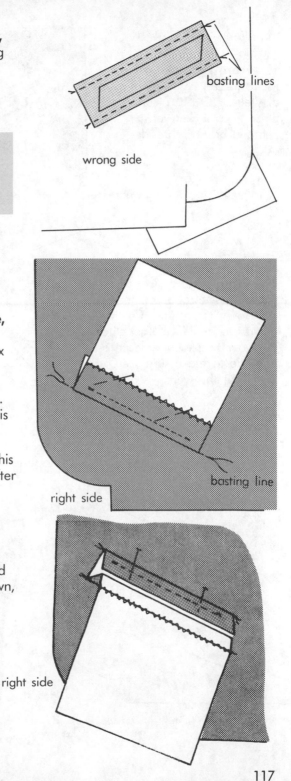

basting lines

wrong side

basting line

right side

right side

117

12. **From right side of jacket,** slash entire length of welts. DO NOT cut through to jacket yet. Remove basting threads.

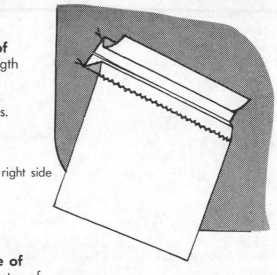

right side

13. **From wrong side of jacket,** cut through center of box to ¾" from end. Cut to corner to middle of **last** stitch. Put your finger underneath as a guide to make sure you don't cut the welts.

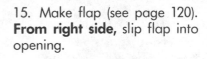

14. Pull everything through to wrong sides. Press.

15. Make flap (see page 120). **From right side,** slip flap into opening.

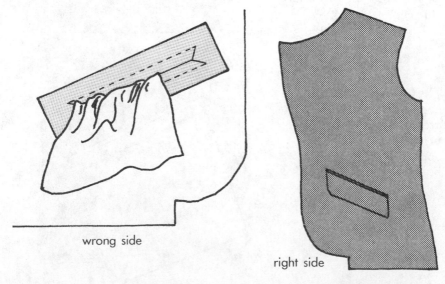

wrong side

right side

16. **On wrong side,** pin pocket flap to welt only.

17. **On wrong side,** stitch flap to top welt.

18. **On wrong side,** bring lining up and stitch across top welt on previous stitching line.

19. Secure triangles at ends of welt. Stitch sides and bottom of pocket as shown. Baste pocket closed to prevent any stretch from occurring during jacket construction.

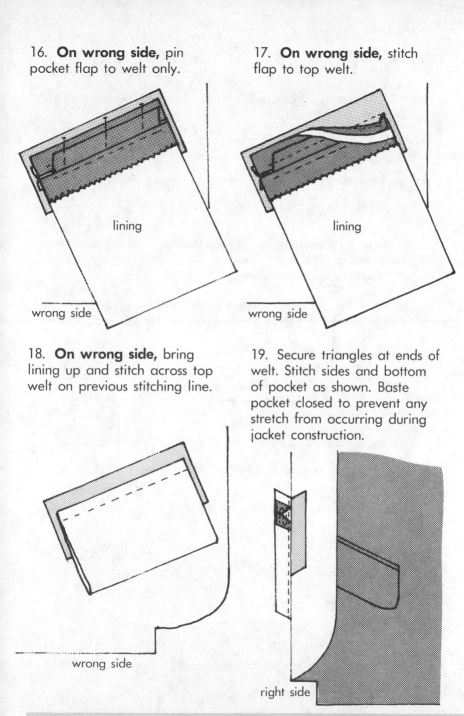

lining

lining

wrong side

wrong side

wrong side

right side

NOTE: Stitch pockets with a round bottom to prevent lint from collecting! Pockets may be shortened by stitching across bottom.

Pocket Flap

1. Cut flap.

2. Fuse lightweight fusible interfacing to wrong side of flap.

3. Cut lining — trim ⅛" off outer edges so lining won't show on finished flap.

4. Pin pocket and lining right sides together. Make sure edges match. (There will be a bubble in the pocket fabric.) Using 20 stitches per inch (so you can trim close), stitch lining to pocket.

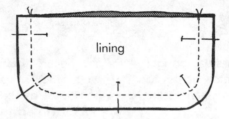

5. Pink seam allowance to ⅛" (or trim to ¼", notch corners).

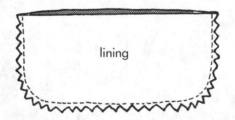

6. Turn and press.

lining pulls to inside
so it won't show

Tailored Patch Pocket

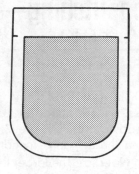

1. **Snip-mark** cut-on facing fold line.

2. **Trim ½" off** seam allowances of interfacing. Fuse to wrong side of pocket.

3. **Fold facing** to wrong side at snips. Press.

4. **Sew lining** to pocket facing, right sides together. Machine baste for 2" at center. (Later, clip the basting to create an opening through which to turn the pocket.)

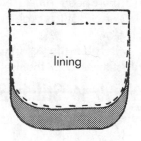

5. **Trim ⅛" off** outer edges of lining. This makes lining smaller so it will pull to inside of finished pocket and not show.

6. **Fold pocket at snips,** right sides together. Match all outer edges and pin in place using lots of pins. There will be a "bubble" in the **pocket** since lining is smaller.

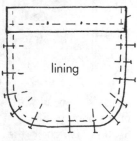

7. **Stitch around pocket** using small stitches.

8. **Press lining** seam allowances toward center of pocket so it will turn better. Trim, grade, notch, slash corners as necessary, or pink around pocket close to seam line.

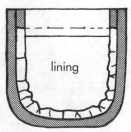

9. **Clip opening** and turn pocket to right side. Press.

10. **Slip a piece of fusible web** into the opening on wrong side and fuse.

11. **Steam baste pocket to jacket** with strips of fusible web. Slip stitch in place by folding jacket back and catching under edge of pocket.

Topstitching—Even You Can Do It

Topstitching } ¼"

Edgestitching } along edge

Thread: Topstitching thread (silk or polyester buttonhole twist) gives a more important looking stitch, and is generally used in top threading only. Or, use 2 strands of sewing thread in top threading going through same needle hole.

Needles: The larger the thread, the larger the needle must be. Size 16-18 (European 100-110) are a must to avoid increased tension. To solve skipped stitch problems, try the Singer® Yellow Band needle and stitch slowly.

Stitch length: A longer stitch (8 stitches/inch) shows up better — small stitches bury themselves in heavier fabrics.

4 Ways to Stitch Straight and Even

presser foot   quilting guide   throat plate guide   topstitching tape

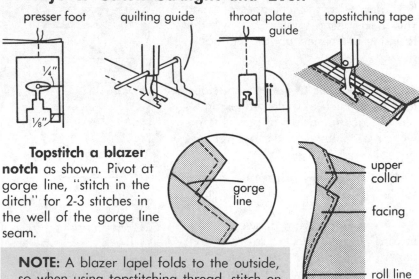

Topstitch a blazer notch as shown. Pivot at gorge line, "stitch in the ditch" for 2-3 stitches in the well of the gorge line seam.

gorge line

upper collar

facing

roll line

jacket right side

NOTE: A blazer lapel folds to the outside, so when using topstitching thread, stitch on upper collar and facing, stop at roll line, tie and bury threads. Flip jacket over and continue stitching on jacket right side.

Tie and bury threads: Pull all threads to wrong side, knot. Touch knot with a dab of Fray Check for extra hold. Thread all ends through a large eye needle, slip needle into seam allowance and bury threads. Clip threads close to fabric at least 1" from knot.

tie

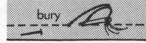

bury

Men's Tailoring — The "Easiest" Method

Our best advice: Since men's tailoring is somewhat different than women's, tell him (and yourself!) that the first jacket will probably be a disaster, but please be patient! Then if this first project is a rousing success it will be a bonus for all! Remember it takes practice sewing for a body — yours or anyone elses.

Men's jackets are different than women's in the following construction techniques:

1. The entire front is usually interfaced
2. Extra layers of interfacing are placed in the front chest and shoulder area
3. Buttonholes are made in the **left** front
4. Hand keyhole or machine made buttonholes are used
5. The jacket back is softer, rarely underlined, and often just partially lined.

Fabrics — Wool tweed is the best choice for a first menswear project, (see No Fail Fabrics, page 16 for other choices) as it is always fashion-right, but is simple to sew, and often reasonable in price.

Pati has decided to only make Ultrasuede jackets for her husband, as that is what he appreciates most, and Ultrasuede is the **easiest** to sew.

Front Interfacing —

Trim ½" from all seams but armhole.

Trim dart out of fusible.

Fuse according to manufacturer's instructions.

Chest Piece —

Cut extra layers of interfacing on bias as shown and fuse in place, one at a time.

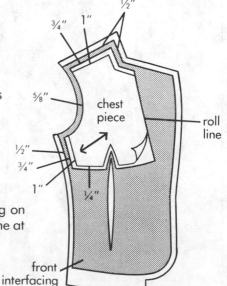

124

Collar — Use this professional tailor's trick to properly shape and shrink roll line of the under collar. Set machine stitch to a very short length — 18 stitches per inch. As you stitch on roll line, stretch the collar away from the roll line by pulling with both hands. This will shrink the roll line. The collar will not lie flat, but will fold on the roll line and automatically stand.

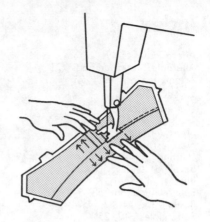

Sleeves — Elbows seem to be the first place to wear out in most fabrics. Cut an oval of fusible knit interfacing with pinking shears (to camouflage the edges). Center over elbow area (tissue fit page 44 to find correct placement) and fuse in place.

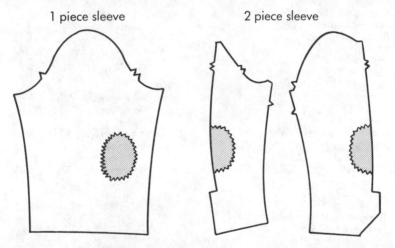

1 piece sleeve   2 piece sleeve

Pockets — Use the Super Duper Double Welt Pocket instructions from page 115 in place of both the inside and outside pocket instructions from most patterns — this method will be easier! Use the "without flap" instructions for inside pockets and sew as many of them as you have time to make. Most men really appreciate additional inside pockets.

Notice we are avoiding discussing custom tailoring for men. If you decide to use traditional custom men's tailoring techniques, read **Men's Tailoring for the Home Sewer**, by Bev Smith. Bev is a menswear expert who has studied with tailors all over the world. We have to thank Bev for teaching us the great welt pocket (see page 115). Write to 1057 Landavo Drive, Escondido, CA 92027. The cost is $5.95.

Index

Other Books from Palmer/Pletsch

Sewing Skinner® Ultrasuede® Fabric by Pati Palmer and Susan Pletsch. 80 pages of instructions to give you the "confidence to cut" into this luxurious fabric. Revised edition copyright © 1976. $4.50.

Mother Pletsch's Painless Sewing with Pretty Pati's Perfect Pattern Primer by Pati Palmer and Susan Pletsch. 136 pages of humor and hassle-free sewing tips. Clear how-to directions and a casual easy-to-read writing style help to reinforce the authors' philosophy that sewing should be fun, fast and easy. You would never think reading a sewing book could be so much fun. Copyright © 1976. $4.95.

Pants for Any Body by Pati Palmer and Susan Pletsch. Newly revised and expanded edition contains 128 pages of the best pant fitting and sewing information available. Copyright © 1982. $5.95.

Sew Big . . . A fashion guide for the fuller figure by Marilyn Thelen. Larger women would like to sew more fashionable apparel. But how? What fabrics should the larger figure wear? In 128 pages, SEW BIG offers solutions to large size problems. Photos, patterns. Wardrobe and accessory information. Alteration instructions. Revised edition copyright © 1981. $5.95.

Sew a Beautiful Wedding by Gail Brown and Karen Dillon. 128 pages of the most concise and current how-to's — from sewing the bridal gown to all the wedding accessories. How to select a pattern to flatter the bride as well as bridesmaids. Sewing techniques for lace, velvet, satin, sheers. Simple-to-make headpieces and veils. Copyright © 1980. $5.95.

Sensational Silk by Gail Brown. 128 page handbook for sewing silk and silk-like fabrics. Complete washing instructions, plus pattern selection, interfacings, sewing on slippery fabrics, special seams and seam finishes, pucker-free zippers and buttonholes, and machine hems. You'll enjoy the designer touches — piping, bias, tucks, pleats, and ruffles. Copyright © 1982. $5.95.

These books are available in local fabric stores or you may order through **Palmer/Pletsch Associates, P.O. Box 8422, Portland, Oregon 97207**. Please add $1.00 for postage and handling. Slightly higher in Canada. Canadian orders please pay in U.S. currency or Canadian equivalent. Prices subject to change.